Rules of the Game

Why Black Men and Women Can't get it together

KEM Publications

www.myspace.com/rulesofthegamebook

Dedication

This book is dedicated to my sons, the better parts of me

Rules of the Game
Why black men and women
Can't get it together

K. Alonzo Hart
Author/Motivational Speaker

K.E.M. Publications

Publisher's Note

This publication is intended to give accurate information in regard to the subject matter. The publisher or author is not engaged in rendering psychological, financial, legal, or other professional services. If expert assistance or advice is needed, the services of a professional should be sought.

Case histories and stories contained in this book have been altered considerably in order to protect privacy. Most often details from similar cases have been reorganized to present one story.

K.E.M Publications
Atlanta, Ga.

www.rulesofthegamebook.com

rulesofthegamebook@yahoo.com

Cover photographs by Jennifer Jewell Macon/Image Control Photography

Contents

Preface

Who am I? I am a product of the very institution that I address in this book, the dysfunctional black family. I am the bastard son of a man who fathered eight or nine kids by about three or four different women during his career as the lead singer of one of the biggest R&B groups in the music industry during the late 60's and 70's. I call myself a "bastard" because that is what I was ever since the day I was born and that is what I'll be the day that I die, a bastard. While my father was singing on stages in front of thousands and being nominated for Grammy awards, I was being raised from one ghetto to the next. While my father was making the ladies scream to the sounds of his sweet tenor voice at four and five years old, I screamed daily from the torture bestowed upon me by my mom's new husband.

This person was extremely jealous of my father's celebrity. Whenever he caught me trying to sing or emulate my father in any way, he would wait until my mother left. Then, he would beat me senseless; strip me down to my underwear, and make me stand outside in the cold West Philadelphia snow. While I shivered and my little fingers and toes turned blue, he would yell and taunt me by saying; *"sing now little motha- fucka, sing now"!* I swear he must have beaten every song out of my little body. My mother told me once that when I was only three years old I used to cry and ask her off and on; "where is my daddy" and like many mothers with new "men" in their lives trying hard to fit a square peg into a round hole, she would tell me, "he's in the other room." She went on to explain how I would correct her and say; "not him, my black daddy." You see the cat she hooked up with was a light-skinned man and I knew the difference. Outside of a father's protection, I was left to fend for myself against the insane abuse of a monster, my mother's new husband.

Even as a child, I guess I knew that things were not right. I went on to suffer awhile at the hands of this individual. As did my mother for that matter, before she finally had enough and moved down south; Still more ghettos but at least away from him. Ironically, this type of child abuse did not turn me into a "child abuser" or some kind of troubled youth. Instead, I absorbed the pain and turned it into understanding; the kind of understanding that can only come from deep suffering. I learned what it meant to be a man and how important a man's role is to his woman and family. I learned that without the man in the home all hell breaks loose; the kind that I walked through as a child and many times much worse. As humble as the beginnings were, this is not to say that I have not tried to improve upon my lot in life. Surely, I have. I have been married for about 12 years. I have children of my own, and thankfully, none of them will ever have to refer to themselves as a bastard. None of them ever suffered through any form of child abuse by my hand or any other. I do not consider my circumstance or myself remotely unique or special. Where I grew up there were hundreds of boys and girls who were fatherless bastards, just as I was.

The problem with being a bastard is that you are forced to constantly figure out life without the wisdom of a father. Therefore, as you grow older you only understand the dynamics that exist between a woman and a man from a mother's point of view. This point of view is often lop-sided and incomplete. Never having the luxury of fatherly guidance, I was forced to learn about the things that make my community sick first hand. Like millions of other black boys in America, growing up without the presence of a father in the home, the streets became a classroom for many of us. By the 1970s, most black families ended up in shambles because of the civil rights movement, the gay rights movement, and the women's rights movement. It was as if the men were either too busy trying to make some "paper," or finally coming to terms with their gay sexual orientation. It seemed like brothas were leaving their homes by the thousands, leaving behind sons and daughters as well as disgruntled wives. It was as if the men simply gave up on their families!

The women on the other hand were sick of being stay-at-home moms. Seemingly, all at once they enrolled in colleges or took on full time jobs in the name of being free and making ends meet. All the while, us kids were sitting around surprised and shocked like, "what just happened"? Many of us became what was commonly known back then as "latch key kids". These are children who had to come home from school and let themselves in with a key provided to them by their mothers and were to remain locked inside until the mothers came home from work. Left to raise ourselves, many neighborhoods turned into ghettos and the streets ran rampant with crime. Young boys without guidance turned to each other for support; often running in "cliques" doing whatever to whomever all in the name of survival and being "cool". The pregnancy rate among young girls without the love of their fathers rose dramatically. Thus fueling what I see today as a growing impatience and intolerance between

between black men and women. When you live and experience the things that make it hard for black men and women to get together. It ain't too hard to write about it. The game I refer to in this book is the game of life, and love between the black man and his woman.

Introduction

The Black American family is one of the world's most sickly institutions. However, before you can analyze the black family you have to first analyze the status of black love relationships. Marriage among blacks in the U.S. has become somewhat of an enigma. Gone are the days when young girls dreamed of becoming brides and young men were groomed to lead families. These once ideal aspirations have slowly given way to the onslaught of hedonism and decadent attitudes of modern culture. The U.S. Census department figures show that 34% of Americans ages 18 to 34 have never been married at all. For African Americans that figure is a whopping 54%. The structure of the black family has undergone a dramatic transformation with each passing generation. One dramatic aspect has been the slow disintegration of the institution of family. Nearly two-thirds of all black marriages end in divorce, and 2 out of 3 African American children will feel the painful collapse of their parents' marriage by the age of 17. One of the changes in family structure over the years has been the increase in single-parent families. In 1970, the number of single-parent families with children under the age of 18 was 3.8 million. Nevertheless, in 2000 women maintained the overwhelming majority of black single-parent families (90.1%). In 2000, 19.2 million children under the age of 18 lived with one parent. 58.2% of them were black children. (Casper, L.M, and J. Fields) Americas Families and Living Arrangements Population Characteristics. United States Census Bureau. 2000.) As a result of these dismal statistics unbalanced relationships between black men and women are the norm. These statistics have made the already weak black family institution vulnerable to feministic ideology and socially deviant behaviors that ultimately have a corrosive effect on black love relationships.

Rule # 1
Black Women: A Balancing Act

Making deals

There is an unsettling trend happening among black women. Many of them end up scraping the bottom of the barrel and making deals these days with men who are for lack of a better word straight up "lames." Out of desperation, these women are forming relationships with these types of men, and in many cases even having their children. Less than twenty years ago a man had to be on his "A- game" in order to pull a quality woman. He had to spit serious game, dress impeccably, have his money situation together, or have a genetically transferable talent athletically or intellectually. Nowadays, women are settling down with men who are not up-to-par just to keep from being lonely during the holiday season. The logic most women espouse is that any man is better than "no man" at all or some other woman's man for that matter. It does not matter if they give birth to a child that is deaf, dumb, crippled, crazy, and blind as a result, of such an ill-fated union. Fear of loneliness appears to be the sole determining factor these days when it comes to black women settling for inferior men. The thought of being alone overrides their natural instincts to be discriminating in the selection of a man. This type of desperate rationale is slowly bringing about the rise of a genetically inferior group of African Americans who will not be able to compete in the world of tomorrow. In other words black women who are settling for men who have nothing to offer genetically, economically or intellectually will be giving birth to bottom- feeders. They are directly handicapping the next generation of African Americans. You see, the game of life is all about survival. A people's ability to compete

15

in their environment usually is the determining factor if that group of people will survive or not. Genetic traits such as talent, intellect, and athletic ability create a tiered order amongst humans. Those who possess them are at the top of that order, thus increasing their odds of not only surviving in the world but also prospering in it.

We must ask the question; what will the future hold for us as an ethnic group of people? Do we even care? As it stands today, blacks are merely breeding children that are more suited for a life of servitude than anything else. Because the law of natural selection still rings true even within the concrete jungle of American society, only the strong survive. Every black man's survival begins and ends with a black woman's choice in a mate.

Too much church?

The black church, as some call it, has been a fixture in the African American community for centuries. It has been within the hallowed halls of this nation's many black churches that most African Americans have been exposed to the idea of "westernized social morality'. However, there has been an over-exposure to church traditions. This has caused many black women to place unrealistic expectations on the very idea of being in a relationship with a man not to mention choosing one to marry. Many women have begun to use the concept of "going to church" as a leveraging tool in their prospective relationships. By this, I mean that in today's society the new career single black woman spends most of her time either on her job or at church. She learns Sunday after

Sunday to do nothing unless she receives direct instructions from G-d or her Pastor. Whether it is purchasing a home, car, making a friend or something as simple as what clothes to wear to work. On the surface, this seems harmless and noble to some degree if not tedious and trivial in some extreme cases. However, she brings this same attitude in a love relationship with a man and many have learned to leverage this "wait on G-d" indoctrination directly against the demands of the men in their lives. By doing this a woman is able to challenge the leadership of her husband simply by invoking G-d into the equation whenever it suits her needs mostly when the man tries to assert his dominance in the relationship.

This sneak attack during a power struggle in a relationship often has a neutralizing affect on the man, simply because G-d is a tough act to follow. I remember once I was invited to a relationship seminar and I was fielding random questions and comments from the audience, which was made up of several intensely opinionated women who were obviously educated, beautiful, and single. One particular woman, a cooperate professional, said that if she were to ever get married that she would have to have equal decision-making power in the relationship and that her husband would never be permitted to have the final word on any issue. The moderator asked her, *"So what if you both do not agree, who then makes the final decision?"* She abruptly said with hands on hips and her cleavage pouring out of her sweater like a fine merlot wine; *"not him, shoot we both are going to have to get on our knees and seek G-d*

17

for an answer and not get up until we do."

Many women have gotten this type of silent protest down to a near art form. The rationale is loosely based on the idea that "I can hear G-d for myself." In many cases men who have found G-d or the Pastor too tough of an act to follow into a competition for the loyalty and faith of his woman have chosen to say: "Since you can hear G-d, for yourself, then you can be by yourself." They simply leave her altogether. However, in these days and times many men have learned to spot these types of woman within a few moments of conversation. Men quickly move on to the next one, which is why nearly all of the churches today are filled to the brim with women, a sprinkle of married men and of course the obligatory effeminate choir directors. The old cliché used to be that if a man wanted to find a good woman all he had to do was go to church. If this cliché has any truth to it then why on earth aren't men packing the pews every Sunday at churches around America?

Why are most black churches made up predominately of black women? This strange dynamic in the black community has been going on for as long as the black church has been in existence. You see, the reason why "real" men often bypass the Christian church is that upon one visit it is easy to see that the social structure that is set up in the church is based on the Pastor being the single male authority figure in the church. He is the direct link to G-d and everyone in the congregation takes all of their cues from him. It just so happens that the majority of the congregation is made up of women who often times worship the ground the Pastor walks on.

The Pastor in the Christian church touches the lives of his parishioners very intimately. He often counsels them on a variety of issues of a deep and personal nature that directly affect the lives of those he leads. Once again, by virtue of the majority of the congregation being made up of women, this type of male leadership has a weird, if not awkward effect on the way the women not only treat the Pastor, but how they relate to other men. Particularly, single black men who happen to visit the church and are not members of the congregation become competition for female attention with the Pastor. This competition is fueled by the tendency to compare any male visitor to the Pastor. It just so happens that black preachers have often been the only recognized leaders in the black community for many years and black women have a soft-side for men who hold power or influence over others particularly over other men. Consequently, when a "real" man comes into a church he immediately understands that he will have to compete with the Pastor for the attention of the women. Now aside from simply grabbing a woman that has caught his attention and pulling her away from the church environment altogether, most men simply do not go and take their chances at the club. Ironically, they often run into the same women that go to church every Sunday. This social disfunctionality hinders black men and women from getting together and getting to know each other on a more earth-based level. I remember once there was a very popular mega church back in the mid 90s the pastor was young handsome and vibrant. He was a fabulous orator. Most of all he was single. The church grew in excess of what has been reported to be at least

5,000 members strong. A more realistic estimation would be around three thousand members. The church was packed wall-to-wall with some of the most beautiful women in the metro area. It seemed as if women came from everywhere just to hear this man "preach." One day the big announcement came that this young single, anointed pastor of this huge congregation of faithful followers was going to settle down and get married. The wedding talk was all the rage. It was a who's who list of attendees. After the grandiosity of the wedding, this mega church of an estimated 5,000 members had shrunk to a reported 500 members seemingly overnight. Moreover, it has never grown to its former glorious size since. This "next big thing" pastor seemed to fall off the religious radar just as quickly as he appeared, like a fallen rock star abandoned by his once loyal army of groupies. He beamed brightly for a moment, then faded quietly into the shadows of mediocrity. Across the country some of the most beautiful black women are rotting on the pews of the churches they attend. They are either eye-balling the pastor hoping to have "him" or hoping and wishing to find a man like him. Many of these women have had men cross their paths that would have made excellent husbands, but because of their loyalties to their churches and pastors, they are unable to take advantage of the opportunities. They cannot bring themselves to believe that these seemingly ordinary men may be the actual ones they need, despite the fact that many of them have prayed desperately for G-d to send them a companion. Black women must learn to balance their desire for spirituality with their desire for the touch and companionship of a man. The situation is not any better for married men in the church either because often the husband must always take a back seat to the Pastor when it comes to spiritual matters.

Married women often use the words of the Pastor to chastise their husbands directly or indirectly. For most men this has an emasculating effect and causes resentment towards the Pastor. The husband feels as if he does not govern his home, but his Pastor does. In churches where married couples attend, the wives often value the opinion of the Pastor over their husbands. Depending on the age, charisma, prominence, and integrity of the Pastor, adultery has often been the result of such admiration of the Pastor by married women. In many black churches today, married black women serve on church committees where they are directly responsible for "serving" the Pastor. For example during many services married women serve the Pastor refreshments such as water and orange juice while he is speaking so that he doesn't go thirsty during a sermon. Some of these same women will go home to their husbands and refuse to serve him with "same" dutifulness because she values her Pastor more than she values her husband. In no way should a married woman give honor to, serve, or admire any man other than her husband or father who raised her from childhood. Married and single women alike who serve and idolize their Pastors are the primary reason why "real" men stay away from the Christian church not because they do not respect G-d but because they do not want their women looking to another man for direction for any reason spiritual or otherwise.

Passive men

The true nature of a black woman is strong and aggressive. Many times this attribute does not balance or compliment black love relationships because ironically black men are also strong-minded and aggressive. In times long past a black woman would intentionally subjugate her aggressive nature in her relationship, so as not to conflict with her man's already dominate nature. However, the more black women buy into the concept of feminism they become less tolerant of being involved in a relationship where they feel compelled to control or restrain their aggressiveness. This in turn creates a clash between the two natures of black men and women.

A black American woman is one of the most demanding women on the planet. Quite simply, they expect a lot from their men, but most of all they have little if any patience for weak men. You can take the most timid black woman and give her a weak black man and she will not respect him. It is almost as if sistas are programmed to respond only to a man who she perceives to be strong. Now this is not to say that a black woman who is desperate for companionship will not settle for a passive man in order to cure her loneliness. She may out of desperation choose a passive man who is available at the time, but this concession does not guarantee that she will have respect for him. It only means that she is desperate. Actually, a black woman who settles for this kind of man out of loneliness will make that man's life a living hell. She will most likely end up ruling him with an iron fist. Though, this is a bad situation for the man it is not any better for her because one thing about black women is that they

22

take no real pleasure in "ruling" their men. This is an equally frustrating proposition for her because eventually she will lose interest in him and will long for a man with a much stronger constitution. Now, when she finally ends up with a man who has a stronger personality, managing that situation can be difficult as well because she constantly challenges his role in the relationship. Sure, the sex can be great, but when it comes down to the business of everyday living, in addition, working together, the struggle over who is going to "lead" the relationship becomes more and more evident. So now, this relationship is filled with constant bickering and fighting, until one of them gives in to the will of the other. Ultimately, dissolving the relationship altogether becomes the only option for peace. By this time, a pregnancy has occurred, thus continuing a never-ending cycle of single parent homes and fatherless children. This is why when I hear men say that they have never had to get physical with their woman at least once during their relationship, I question their truthfulness. I question it because this is hard to believe, considering the fact that it is definitely within a black woman's nature to push her man to that point eventually. I say this because the black woman's disdain for weak men will often cause them to wonder what type of man she is dealing with, especially, if a considerable amount of time has elapsed in the relationship and she has yet to see him loose his cool. It is not beyond a black woman to pick a fight with her man just to see if he has "balls" or not. The reason for this kind of provoking behavior is that a black woman who questions her man's "manhood" will ultimately threaten it just to see if he is going to stand his ground.

Any man who fails to check his woman when she challenges his manhood will end up looking "weak" in her eyes and can thus expect nearly any form of disrespectful behavior in the future. A woman will ultimately deal with a man according to her experiences with other men in her life whether they were absent, weak, fathers or "hen pecked" boyfriends. She will deal with her man the same way she dealt with them until he demands that she treat him differently.

When a man hits his woman

Domestic violence in intimate relationships between men and women, unfortunately, is as about as common in America as the common cold. In addition, like the common cold, most people and their relationships are not immune to domestic violence. Still, this is a hot button issue for most women and rightfully so because in most cases they are the victims of this kind of abuse. However, women need to realize that men who claim that they would never hit a woman for any reason are most likely lying. I would warn that men who say this are more prone to actually "kill" you than anything else. I say this because logically if your man is human he is capable of any kind of behavior including violence. I mean, the average person has a normal amount of patience and tolerance, but say you walk up and spit in his face, more than likely he is going to smack the crap out of you, cuff you or something. Now, there are some people who are "least likely" to commit certain acts, which is primarily based on individual personality make-up more so than any kind of moral code or consciousness. Still conventional wisdom dictates that a man who says what he will "never" do is most likely capable of doing anything. So this ushers in the age-old question, "Should a man ever hit his woman?" This is a theoretical question because in theory, the short answer would be "no" but because most relationships are not lived out in a "theoretical" sense, one must change the question to, should a man ever "have" to hit his woman? Once again, the answer is "no." He should not have to hit his woman, but depending on her upbringing or lack thereof, this may be an unfair question to ask. I say this because in today's society men have become accustomed to suppressing their natural aggressive nature in order to fit into society's ever-changing ideas of what is and what is not appropriate social behavior. In contrast, women today are encouraged to become more "aggressive" and assertive, thus creating a more adversarial relationship. The answer to the question is that a man should not "have" to get physical with a woman who was raised by a father who gave her the proper "physical chastisement" that she deserved when she was a child.

If a husband's words are not enough to bring his woman into compliance with his leadership then his fist will only manage to break her spirit as well as her heart. You see a "pimp" has to break the will and spirit of his woman so that she will use her body to turn him a profit. Therefore, from time to time he has to lay his hands on her in order to drive his message of compliance home. They both are the obvious products of broken homes so she interprets his physical abuse as love and concern. Thus, she complies with her pimp's wishes whenever he beats her. In a perfect world, a husband should be able to use his words to keep his house in order. However, we do not live in a perfect world instead we live in a time where the majority of black women come from the same broken homes as black men do. In these homes, the absence of male authority and leadership often inspire future relationships that imitate more of a "pimp and bitch" situation rather than a "husband and wife" marriage. Therefore, physical altercations between the black man and his woman is more about the misinterpretation of one's role in the relationship and not likely to be solved by politically-correct driven ideals. Instead, the reinstatement of the black man as the sole authority in the home is the only remedy that can bring balance back to black love relationships and order to black families. The black woman must "allow" this reinstatement to take place by choosing to compliment her man's authority rather than demand that he share it. When a black woman grows up in a home without a father she views any man trying to assert his authority over her as an "intrusion" and feels insulted at any form of correction or criticism that he directs towards her. This is why black men must become the leaders of their families once again, so that they can become fathers to both their sons and daughters. Hence, daughters will learn to embrace black manhood and cooperate with it at a much earlier age.

A daughter learns how to co-exist with a man by virtue of her relationship with her dad. Therefore, it is the father's duty to chastise both his sons and daughters, as well. When a little girl receives both verbal and physical chastisement from her father, she learns how to internalize it as a lesson or correction not simply abuse. She does not internalize it as abuse because, excluding a dysfunctional household, her chastisement was done in love with her best interests in mind. She learns how to communicate respectfully with her father thus; she does the same with her husband. When she says something out of line or disrespectful, her father should be the first to correct her on the matter. If he does not when she gets married, her husband will find much difficulty establishing his leadership in the home. Therefore, these lessons of respecting male leadership need to begin in the daughter's childhood home first.

Father knows best

The problem with all of this is that historically in the black community men have not always stayed home to help rear their children. Those that did usually were unsure of how to relate to their daughters outside of giving hugs and kisses. These confused men often did not participate in physically chastising their daughters either, instead leaving the responsibility strictly to the mother. This kind of ambivalent attitude towards raising daughters has produced a generation of black women who have no idea how to relate to men outside of giving up the "booty", thus, contributing to the growing divide and hostility that exists today between black men and women.

So, when a black woman tells her man, "you don't talk to me that way, my own father didn't do this or that", you had better believe her because chances are she is telling the truth. This is precisely part of the problem. A woman who comes into a marriage with no previous experience with being molded, shaped, loved and

27

chastised by her father is going to be unprepared to deal with the demands placed on her by her new husband. Likewise, the new husband is going to have his hands full trying to figure out how best to fill in the blanks left by her parents. A woman learns how to be a loyal wife to her husband by first learning how to be loyal to her father. Daughters at an early age should be aware that they are under the strict authority of their father.

By creating this sense of awareness parents give the child her first actual sense of "belonging" to a man in a healthy loving relationship. The daughter then says to herself, "I am my father's" and this becomes a major part of her identity. She develops her self-worth through this relationship. The father gives the daughter love, attention, and protection. In return, the daughter gives her father loyalty. This mutual exchange enables the daughter to respect her father's authority over her life, not resent it. Daughters who rebel against their fathers' authority often resent them because they see or feel hypocrisy, neglect, abuse, and weakness in them. A woman's loyalty to her husband should not be based on an idea of "perfection," but instead respect, stability, in addition, security. She learns how to love her husband by first understanding the many imperfections of her father.

Through this type of submission and loyalty, the woman finds her purpose. I believe this to be true because the woman is the first teacher of the child. Thus, children learn how to follow and submit to authority by following the example set forth by the mother. However, in today's society, particularly among blacks, this type of relationship between men and women is slowly becoming more and more unrealistic. Primarily, because men and women in the black community are increasingly beginning to see each other as rivals instead of mates.

Could black women be the problem?

For many years black men have been labeled as the entire reason why black families and love relationships are failing. However, just how much of a role do black women play in this sad story? Are we to believe that sistas are blameless? Of course not! The black woman in America is praised by white America for her educational, political, and economic advancements, while on the other hand, black men are feared. Educated black women are viewed by the larger white society as some sort of harmless, asexual matriarchs. While educated black men simply are labeled as militant and dangerous.

Instead of creating strong families, black men and women are fighting over the economic scraps thrown to them from the social dinner table of white folk. By economic scraps, I mean policies such as "affirmative-action," which black and white women have long since benefited from more often than black men, but with a far greater divisive effect on the black community as a whole. Black men and women in America are beginning to live in two different world's drifting further and further apart, having less and less in common, all within the same society. This kind of social drift between black men and women has a distinct effect on how they both not only view each other, but how they see themselves as well. In a society where a black woman is praised for being

29

"better" than her man, it is no surprise that, eventually over a period of time, she will begin to see herself through the eyes of her admirers, rather than through the eyes of the men in her community. This "positive" self-image with an emphasis on self-reliance is wreaking havoc on black love relationships because it conflicts with the notion of "submission" on behalf of the woman, which is imperative to the future success of the black family. It is imperative because the American black male is probably one of the most obstinate types of men on the planet. His hyper-masculinity is seemingly hardwired into his very being. Therefore, when you combine the concepts of the new "independent-black woman" with the naturally "obstinate-hyper-masculine" black man, you have a serious problem because both cancel each other out. The black family will cease to exist without the black man's leadership because a generation of black kids will grow into adulthood never truly understanding how to "follow" and submit to the concept of authority.

Matriarchy: the slow poison

There have been two main social movements in American culture that have emasculated black men. American culture historically prevented the exercise of his authority over his family. The Matriarchal family system was introduced to the American black by the institution of slavery and perpetuated by the Women's liberation movement of the 1970's. The black family in America has been crippled and poisoned by an imposed "Matriarchal" family system that was created during slavery in order to destabilize and undermine the authority of the "father" in his home. The chief characteristic of the Matriarchal family is the dominant role of the wife. Matriarchal women usually have strong personalities, a high degree of self-determination, and a strong desire to be the family leader. American law did not recognize slave marriages and family ties therefore; slave owners were free to sell husbands from wives, parents from children, and brothers from sisters. Many wealthy slaveholders had several plantations and often times' shuffled slaves from plantation to plantation, splitting up families indefinitely in the process. Most estimates indicate that at least 10 to 20 percent of slave marriages were destroyed by sale. The sale of children from parents was even more common. Because of the sale or death of a father or mother, over a third of all slave children grew up in households from which one or both parents were absent. This type of insidious, inhumane disregard for the lives of people and their families often left the women alone without a husband, usually with her children unprotected, totally at the mercy of a cruel master and American social order.

You see this is where the "split" began. The black woman by default became the head of the family because she found herself becoming less and less dependent on the leadership and protection of her husband seeing that he had no power to lead his family out of the bondage of slavery. Often times in order to hammer into the mind of the male slave that he was nothing, the slave master would visit the slave quarters late in the evening, enter a prospective slave cabin, and rape the wife or daughter of any male slave of his choosing. Often the male slave was made to watch as the slave owner repeatedly raped his wife with impunity. As a result, the black man was rendered powerless and insignificant not only in his house, but in the one place where all men want to feel significant, in the eyes and heart of his woman. As a result, the social role of the husband and father has become an odd and obscure concept among the African American. We are witnessing today firsthand the tragic results of a black male culture seeking a masculine identity within an illegitimate matriarchal family system where fathers are virtually absent from the home and young men model themselves after hip-hop artists and athletes. All while the divorced and matriarchal single-parent culture finds its way deeper into the minds of black people. The Matriarchal family system among African Americans was not born from the free will of black people. It came from the hateful womb of the American social order. It is the bastard child of slavery. The dysfunctional and problematic relationship that exist between black men and women today is rooted in this very troubled and mired social history of the African in America.

Rule #2
Just Say "No" to Feminism

"The day will come when men will recognize a woman as his peer, not only at the fireside, but in councils of the nation. Then, and not until then, will there be the perfect comradeship, the ideal union between the sexes that shall result in the highest development of the race." — **Susan B. Anthony**

The woman responsible for giving birth to the new "feminist" mindset in America was a woman by the name of Betty Friedan. Friedan was born Betty Naomi Goldstein in Peoria, Illinois on February 4, 1921. Ironically, one year after women were legally allowed to vote. Before founding the National Organization for Women in 1966 Friedan was a college educated disgruntled housewife, who while disenchanted with the traditional "lily white" nuclear family structure, got so bored that she formulated a feminist dogma that would change how women in America viewed themselves, including black women whom she absolutely had nothing in common with whatsoever.

The scope of Friedan's feminist thought was and still is that "all women are oppressed". Her radical theories focused on liberating women from their roles as wives and mothers. In her view, these roles were not healthy for women and that all women should seek an identity outside of their families. In other words Friedan was teaching women to become more individualistic and materialistic and less maternal. Ever since the release of Betty Friedan's book entitled *The Feminine Mystique*, white feminists have influenced black women to see themselves outside of black men. Black women for years have bought into the doctrine of feminism in America. Betty Friedan is considered the chief architect of contemporary feminist thought and ideology. Her book explains how women were oppressed, and that they should be sexually liberated and pursue career goals outside of the home. However, Friedan was not directing her opinions at black women, who at the time were in a fight to save their families from a perpetual dysfunctionality that was due to the residue of slavery in America.

The Black woman did not need liberation from her man. She needed to unite with him. Nevertheless, gullible black activist women blindly took up the banner of feminism in America using the lack of female leadership within the Civil Rights movement and the Black Liberation Movement in the sixties as an excuse to join arms with white feminists against their black men. As a result, a deeper divide between black men and women was becoming wider by the minute. Zealous black female activists, anxious to pump their fists, ultimately began to form Black feminist organizations that did nothing more than mimic white feminist organizations. These organizations only served to bolster the white feminist political agenda on Capitol Hill by giving white feminists the ability to piggy-back on the Civil Rights movement, thus expanding their feminist agenda by equating their "so-called" white woman's struggle with that of African Americans.

Friedan states:
"We can no longer ignore that voice within women that says: 'I want something more than my husband and my children and my house. '" She goes on to say, It is urgent to understand how the very condition of being a housewife can create a sense of emptiness, non-existence, nothingness in women. There are aspects of the housewife role that make it almost impossible for a woman of adult intelligence to retain a sense of human identity, the firm core of self or "I" without which a human being, man or woman, is not truly alive. For women of ability, in America today, I am convinced that there is something about the housewife state itself that is dangerous. For what it has done or learned by one

The Result of Black Feminism

one class of women becomes, by virtue of their common womanhood, the property of all women."— Elizabeth Blackwell

Black feminism in America has never truly taken root in the black community because it is illogical and does not correspond to the reality of the black family experience. Instead, feminism in the black community is more of a minor subculture usually made up of black lesbians along with disgruntled black female professionals fed up with being alone. Bottom-line, black folks, do not have the luxury of embracing that kind of white woman's crap when faced with so many other ills and challenges, namely trying to make the whole "family-thing" work as an ethnic group. Still, one cannot underestimate the affects of Black Feminism on the black community. Black feminism provides a place of refuge for women who need to feel empowered in their loneliness. These kinds of women have come up with all kinds of feminist logic in order to justify the existence of being alone. Such philosophical perspectives include sayings such as, "I don't need a man, I'm fine all by myself," or "I don't need a man to take care of me." Any woman who quotes this kind of "feel-good" rationale is desperately trying to make sense out of a senseless situation. It is senseless for any woman to be alone because she does not have to be alone. All she needs to do is learn how to manage her true nature as a black woman so that it cooperates and compliments the manhood of black men. Black women are going to have to start making concessions or the future does not look too bright for the black family. Current statistics reveal that the whole notion of the so - called black family is in jeopardy of not existing in the near future. Let us examine what black feminism has contributed to the black community. Today the number of children born into a black marriage averages less than 0.9 children per marriage. "The birthrates of black married women have fallen so sharply that absent out of-wedlock childbearing; the African American population would not only fail to reproduce itself, but would rapidly die off." (The Abolition of Marriage, by Maggie Gallagher p. 120, citing Reynolds Forley, "After the Starting Line: Blacks and Women in an Uphill Pace," Demography 25, no. 4 (November 1988): 487, Figure 6).

"'Exposure to single motherhood at some point during adolescence increases the risk [of a daughter's later becoming a single mother] by nearly [150 percent] for whites and by about 100 percent for blacks.'"(Sara S. McLanahan, "Family Structure and Dependency: Reality Transitions to Female Household Headship," Demography 25, Feb., 1988, 1-16. Cited in Amneus, The Garbage Generation, page 240)
The Joint Center for Political and Economic Studies reports that by the age of 30, 81 percent of white women and 77 percent of Hispanics and Asians will marry, but that only 52 percent of Black women will marry by that age. Black women are also the least likely to re-marry following divorce. Only 32 percent of Black women will get married again within five years of divorce.

That figure is 58 percent for White women and 44 percent for Hispanic women.

According to the Center for Disease Control's May 24, 2001 health statistics, non-Hispanic black women are less likely than other women to remain in a first marriage, to make the transition from separation to divorce, to remarry, and to remain in a remarriage. According to the Joint Center for Political and Economic Studies in Washington, the percentage of black women who are married declined from 62 percent in 1950 to 36 percent in 2000.

Researcher, Bell-Hooks, asserts that it could be a powerful act of defiance for Black women to choose to be with White men. According to the U.S. Census Bureau, the number of black female/white male marriages remained relatively static between 1960 and 1980, increasing from 26,000 to 27,000. However, by 2000, the number had jumped to 80,000.

Black Manhood vs. Black Feminist

Black feminists fail to realize is that 400 years of slavery could not eradicate the unique African American male hyper-masculine ego. It is extremely unlikely that black American men will ever accept or respect feminism in any way shape or form. Unlike white men who are slowly, becoming domesticated and feminized by their white feminist counterparts, black men are not so easily changed. In a face-off between Black feminist and Black manhood, brothas will win easily because they will simply choose a woman who is able to conform to his nature rather than deal with one who is contrary to it. No matter what his lot in life, a black American male believes in almost a supernatural way that he is the head of his woman, without question. This belief is a non-negotiable part of his very being. It is simply his way.

Career vs. Man

A woman who is very absorbed in her occupation or career should weigh the idea of marriage very carefully because the very idea of having a career is a marriage of sorts. The culture of corporate America often demands that a woman be aggressive. However, the same aggressive quality that makes her an asset to the company often is a liability in her love-marriage. In a marriage she generally is not the "leader," instead she is expected to be the follower of her husband submitting herself to his leadership. This is in stark contrast to the leadership opportunities that many female executives have on the job. A natural law governs a woman's role in the home. This is the law of nature or a woman's maternal law, which requires her to be the primary care-giver and teacher to her children. In theory, nothing is supposed to usurp a woman's natural law of maternity. Considering this, a woman should contemplate and determine whether her greatest desire is to excel in the corporate world before deciding upon the issue of marriage. If a woman's greatest ambition is career advancement through the corporate ranks, then she is better off unmarried until she is able to balance her career life and a potential married life. On the other hand, if a woman's greater desire is to be a wife first, then she should marry because women who wish for marriage but choose career first, end up becoming serial daters never having the time to explore in depth any particular relationship. By the time this kind of woman feels as if she has found Mr. Right, he has already lost interest due to her lack of availability and external career obligations and responsibilities. In addition, a woman who is attracted to marriage but caught up in the day-to-day demands of her career will often become unreliable, unfocused, and unsatisfied with the ultimate direction of her life.

What most women fail to realize is that it takes just as much energy, dedication, and fortitude to cultivate a successful career as it does a marriage. When a woman chooses to postpone marriage in favor of career advancement she unknowingly is, still choosing to be "married" she is just replacing the bridegroom with the "boardroom" or the classroom. The woman still has to go to school and spend a lot of time in the classroom learning how to be a good and professional worker. Once she graduates, she has to submit to the policies and procedures of her employer. No matter how qualified she is, and most of all no matter how high she rises in that corporation she will never reach a level of full "equality" with the owner(s) of that business. Though she may rise to a level where her opinion is respected, she still will never stand on "equal" footing with her employer. Still, many women go full steam ahead with the pursuit of their careers, fully aware of this fact. They are ready and willing to act professionally at all times, keep a neat clean appearance in accordance to that business's dress code, show up to work on time, and refrain from insubordinate actions that may cause their termination.

These women usually always speak to their boss's with the utmost of respect, no matter how rude and obnoxious said employer may be. When interviewing for career jobs most of these women are more than prepared to be turned downed or outright rejected in favor of a more qualified applicant that may appear to be more attractive to the corporation. They handle this type of rejection with dignity and determination and push onward toward the next interview.

In a marriage, women should also apply this kind of work ethic to becoming good wives. A marriage takes a lot of work and needs plenty of time to grow and mature. The dynamics in a marriage are similar to a career or job. On a job, there can only be one true leader. A woman who expects or demands equality in a relationship is a fool because equality in its idealized "American" form is a myth. Therefore, it does not exist. Once a woman chooses to enter a marital relationship, she must realize that she is in effect choosing a leader who will "lead" their family. Therefore, she must respect and trust him as her leader. The only difference between a married woman and the professional woman is that the professional does not realize that she is just as married to her job as the married woman is to her husband. They both follow the same set of rules of submission and cooperation just under different circumstances.

Rule #3
Four Kinds of Women

Because of the perpetual dysfunctionality of the black family, deviant sub-groups have formed along the way. These groups are a direct reflection of the inconsistency of black family life in America. They represent the kind of socially deviant attitudes that can occur within any group of people, where accountability and social responsibility are absent combined with no "real" organized family structure. For years, women have complained that "good men" are hard to find, well in today's society the same can be said about a woman.

Women can be divided into four major groups: "Queen B's," "Hoes," "Freaks," and "Wives." Now in truth, virtually all women possess attributes of each; however, some women tend to bend more to one or the other depending on natural personality, upbringing, and environment. The highest status among the four is the "Wife" status. Most men prefer this status to the other three categories. Because, no matter what, every man wants a woman in his life that is responsible, loyal, and nurturing to his needs. Underneath the hardcore thug exterior of many guys, this type of woman is unanimously the woman of choice. The key to any man understanding just what type of woman he is dealing with is to pinpoint which group she happens to belong. Many brothas have no idea how to approach a woman because they often times do not realize her classification before they start a conversation with her. It is extremely important that men learn how to assess the woman that he has his attention on from afar before he gets too close to her. For instance, some guys approach a woman and try to play the "Mack" role on her right from the start.

However, depending on her classification he may just be making a fool out of himself and wasting his time. All women are as different from one another as night and day. They all have a particular group they belong to and it is up to the man to figure out whether he is dealing with a "Queen B," "Hoe," "Freak," or a future "Wife."

Queen B

Primarily, the academic term "bitch" describes a female dog. The female dog is very independent and moody. She shows little, if no, loyalty to one male dog when she is in "heat" and she will mate with any male dog that happens to jump the fence. Often times several male dogs will mate with the same female while she is in heat. If her breeding is not monitored it is almost impossible to tell what male dog in the neighborhood sired her pups. However, she has little, if no, real tolerance for male dogs when she is not in "heat." Female dogs that are not ready to mate often fight other male dogs that try to mate with them out of season. The Alpha female or "Queen Female" fights off interested males because she has no use for them during this period. She is content going it alone until her next heat cycle.

This is the nature of the "Queen B." This is the first group of women that I will discuss. This type of woman is fiercely independent and all too willing to go it alone to prove that she is self-sufficient. Every man should know when he is dealing with this kind of woman because in the beginning stages of a relationship she is usually on her best behavior trying hard to make a good impression. However, it does not take long for her true colors to show.

44

So, a little bit of patience may go a long way when trying to figure out this kind of woman. Her conversation is usually intriguing and she is quite capable of winning a man over at times with her uncanny ability to match wits with him. Often times, the sex is extremely good because these independent women store up massive amounts of aggressive energy and pent up frustration. However, a woman who falls in this category lacks one key quality that men usually will not negotiate, and that quality is "submission." This woman cannot fathom the idea of submitting to a man. She would just as soon put a bullet between his eyes, than acknowledge him as her "Leader." This woman preaches a message of self-reliance, loud and strong to any woman that will hear. Contrary to what men consider a woman's nature, she claims that she does not need a man to make her a whole person, when in fact beneath her feminist exterior her true desires are exactly the opposite.

You see a "Queen B" is not a "B" because she learned to be that way. She is who she is because she was born frustrated with her own power and strength. She is aware that she is strong and capable of surviving on her own, yet she still desires male companionship and attention. From the day she was born, she had an opinion, an alternative point of view because she was the "alpha female" amongst her peer groups. These women have an uncanny ability to see through the crap that most people hand out. If they grew up hard, they can take their personal tragedies and turn them into ammunition against their enemies.

During life, she learned how to compete at nearly every level. Whether it was kickball in grade school or a

45

student government seat in college. She was a worthy opponent and successful in nearly all of her competitive endeavors except when it came to the opposite sex. In such an arena her power, intelligence, wit, and competitive spirit did not serve her well at all. Instead, they handicapped her efforts to capture the attention of men. On every front, she lost out to the girls who fawned all over the masculinity of the guys on campus. Her bright ideas paled in comparison to their flattering tongues that boosted the egos of the boys in the locker room.

This woman has no interest in boosting a man's ego because she feels that, though she is attracted to him she is no less than his equal. As each year passes by this young woman becomes more and more apathetic to the idea of love and romance. Eventually, she begins to embrace feministic ideology that compels her to love herself. Slowly but surely, after each failed relationship she grows weary of operating in a world with "two left feet" she comes to the realization that it is better to be a "Queen B" with money rather than a broke-chick without a man. The focus of nearly all of her energy goes to her career and education, thus, creating the ever-popular alarmist theory that there is some sort of "man shortage" in the black community, when in fact, these kinds of women often choose career over love.

Many of these types of women are very demanding of their male counterparts. They usually have and extensively long laundry list of demands that they use to evaluate potential mates. These lists are usually both unrealistic and idealistic. They do not reflect any real sense of compassion and softness that most men expect from a woman. Instead, these lists are more like rigid rules and regulations meant to send the message

46

that she's the boss, and no man is going to determine the who, what, where, or when, as it pertains to any future relations between them. Most of these women absolutely detest men who expect them to play a passive role in the relationship. The mere mention of the word "submission" draws their fierce rebellion. In essence, these women cannot stomach the notion of taking a passive role in a relationship. However, the internal conflict within, usually arises when her desire to lead and her instinct for male companionship collide. This is nothing but plain old frustration, and this kind of frustration leads many women to question whether or not the love of a man is even worth it. This is why there are so many single people running around town and running away from marriage. Black men and women are frustrated with each other, so it causes them both to fear the other and shun the institution of marriage altogether.

Undercover

Men who end up with a woman who all of a sudden decides that she wants to try and flip the script on him by changing the power dynamic in the relationship is a common occurrence in many relationships. This usually happens to lesser men who often are easily manipulated by a woman with a stronger game and personality. However, not all hope is lost for those men out there trying hard to avoid these types of situations. First, there are always signs that may indicate whether you have an undercover "B" on your hands. Many women have become quite adept at concealing their true "Queen B" nature from a man at least in the beginning of a prospective relationship. The efforts that many women will go through at times can be comical. These women often pretend to be polite, unobtrusive, cuddly, and even submissive. All of these efforts to the trained eye are very easy to see through because the behaviors are obviously contrived, awkward, and downright plastic at times. Still many women will play this fake role down to the wire if necessary to pull a man of her choice. Often times these attempts to lure a man into a loving relationship are very unsuccessful simply because during the process many women just cannot stand the fact they are being made to feel like they have to act submissive in order to get a man so they simply give up. Now don't get things twisted many women who have the Queen B mindset have the endurance to play this kind of game extremely well. Many of these women talk a good game at the onset of a possible relationship this is why it is important for men to pay close attention to both her overt and subtle responses when certain request of her time and attention are made. For example, if you are watching television ask her to bring you something to drink.

Now a well-schooled "B" is going to pass this first test with flying-colors the first few times. After the relationship gains a small amount of tenure you, many notice subtle changes in her responses to the same request. She may begin to demonstrate the "silent protest," by this I mean that when you initially asked her to bring you something to drink she would do so with gladness and an almost girlish eagerness to please. She always made sure your drink was cold and ready. Now she begins to display a slightly different response.

She now brings the drink with no ice, until finally when she can no longer keep up the charade she blurts out a few familiar remarks, "I am not your momma and this ain't no restaurant" or the all time classic Queen B comeback "you don't have no maid service around here!" If on the first date when you take her out to a nice restaurant she starts the evening by ordering the most expensive dish on the menu you may be dealing with a "B."

If she orders the most expensive item on the menu this is an indication that she is self-centered and interested in getting all she can out of the evening at the expense of your generosity. After you have taken her out a couple of times and you notice that each time she has never offered to pay for your meal once again you may be dealing with a Queen B. The logic behind this is that once a woman understands that you care enough about her to make sure that she is never wanting for food while she is in your company she "should" show her appreciation by demonstrating her willingness to return the same kind of gesture reassuring you that she is concerned for your well being as well. Now having said this I do realize that some women may not be financially capable of matching their male counterpart's romantic gestures dollar for dollar. However, even if she is a broke chick McDonald's is always open. In other words, there is simply no excuse whatsoever for a woman to receive from a man continually without giving back in return in some way shape or form.

Some men like to shower their women with gifts and at first glance, there is nothing wrong with doing this especially if you have the financial wherewithal to do it. However, there is in fact a limit to everything. Once again, many "square dudes" often find themselves getting hustled by "Queen B's" everyday. These kinds of men obviously have the financial means to purchase expensive gifts for their women however; they lack common sense and discretion. Their desire to want to appear as a "baller" often blinds them to the fact that they are being used indiscriminately for their resources. Any woman can spot a man like this a mile away. Here is what you should look out for: If your girl only gives you gifts on special occasions, such as your birthday and holidays, you may have a serious problem on your hands. The reason I say this is that a woman truly "down" and in love with her man generally wants to do things for him "just because." If your lady is not giving you "just because" gifts, then she is not in love with you at all. She is just with you for whatever reason, most likely because you may have more resources financial or otherwise, than the other guys that are lobbying for her attention. A woman who gives gifts to her man exclusively on special occasions is stringing him along in order to keep him interested, as well as keeping up the appearance of being "attentive".

All these men are checking me out

Getting attention is another characteristic of a Queen B. This woman has to be recognized especially by men. Sometimes she cannot mask her compulsive desire for attention. For instance, let's say you are walking through the mall together; this kind of woman is always concerned with who is checking her out. Some women trying to mask their arrogance will make comments such as, *"what is that guy looking at, doesn't he see that I'm with you?"* Others who are more obvious will make every attempt to catch the eyes of every strange man in the mall. Many of these types of women have to throw on make-up and a pair of tight jeans to go almost anywhere. If your woman is like this, chances are you may be dealing with an undercover "B." Let's say you and your lady want to take a nice stroll on the beach. This is a good opportunity for you to sit back and observe just how she prepares to go on this particular outing. Now depending on whether you are going to a private beach where there are few, if any, people or a densely populated public beach, your woman will adjust her wardrobe to fit either case. Does she wear a long t-shirt over her swimsuit when going to a public beach where there are several hundred to several thousand people? If she does, she is trying to demonstrate to you that her swimwear is for you to see and for her to swim in and she is not interested in parading herself around for other men to gawk at while she is strolling along with you. On the other hand, if she pulls out the skimpiest two-piece thong set that she can find in the closet and attempts to walk hand in hand with you, she is more interested in receiving the attention of other men on the beach. Many men proclaim that they do not mind if their girl displays herself in public half-naked on their arm so long as other men know that she is taken. These deluded men go as far as to say that by allowing their woman to wear such "skimpy" clothing demonstrates that they are secure enough in their relationship to not be jealous but to be flattered! This is self-deception!

If these brothas really feel that secure about parading their woman around half-naked before other men, then they may as well take her up to the local strip club because at least in that environment she can get paid to be seen by other men.

Here is the logic. If a woman is too proud to take her clothes off for money in a strip club, then common-sense would dictate that she shouldn't be comfortable prancing around half-naked in public places while in her man's presence. So why would a woman insist upon dressing in a sexually alluring manner while in public with her man? I will tell you why. It is because she is actually using her unsuspecting boyfriend, fiancé, and or husband to ward off those undesirable men who would normally harass and bother her even if she were single. However, her style of dress sends the message to other more suitable men that she is indeed available and interested in receiving attention from a possible "Mr. Right" to replace her naive "Mr. Right Now."

Whose money is it?

If you are in a relationship with a woman who works a regular, nine-to-five there are a few things, you should watch very closely when it comes to the issue of finances. If your woman makes a point to keep reminding you that the money she makes is "her money," you may be dealing with a "Queen B," this kind of woman always has to be in control and feels that depending on a man for her finances is unacceptable. However, she takes it to another level by using her financial security as a means to dictate the terms of the relationship. A financially secure woman is not necessarily a "Queen B."

What makes her a "B" is whether she uses her financial status as a form of advantage in a relationship. Initially, when meeting a woman like this, men are not ready to deal with her independence. So, many times they end up "getting played" for sex and companionship. A woman in this case will often buy expensive gifts for her new man in order to reel him. She may find out what he likes materially. If he likes to shoot pool, then she will purchase a pool table and invite him over hoping that he will get attached to that particular recreational convenience. If he needs a car, she will allow him to drive hers or if she is financially capable, purchase one for him (in her name of course). She will do all of these things in order to keep him in her space. Now normally, these tactics generally work on men who are between jobs, have no job, or are without transportation. These types of "needy" men are prime candidates for these women.

Some women in this category will purchase a home and stay in it all by her lonesome, just to prove that she is an independent woman who does not need to wait on a man to buy a residential family home. Good advice for any man who is dating a financially secure woman who has her own home is to never move in with her on a permanent basis. Spending nights and weekends or maybe even moving in on a temporary basis can be dangerous ground as well. One of the cardinal sins that some men make is to move in with a woman who already has her own apartment or house. A man should never ever do this. Men who lower themselves to do such a thing should be prepared to be constantly reminded by her that the roof over his head is not his own, but instead

instead it belongs to her. During a fight or argument women in this scenario love to bring up the fact that they bought or acquired the home without the man's assistance and do not need his presence to maintain it. This has an embarrassing, neutralizing effect on men who try to assert themselves while living with these women. The rationale behind all of this is simple; men are by nature territorial and often-lay claim to space or spaces they occupy. Usually chaos breaks loose when a man tries to assume a leadership role in his girlfriend's crib. It breaks loose because the man's territorial behavior rubs against her independent nature. It is almost like adding gasoline to fire. An explosion is bound to happen. So you see, in these kinds of situations you may end up being "the guy" living in a house with this woman, but you will never be the "the man of the house" by virtue of that fact that the space belonged to that woman first. My suggestion is that if you find yourself madly in love with a woman who already has a place of her own and wish to marry her, the first thing you should do is go out and find a comparable living space for the both of you. Afterwards, she needs to sell or rent out her house and move in with you. If she absolutely refuses to sell her house and follow your lead, then you should consider ending the relationship and go about the business of finding a

woman who is more willing to follow you. A man should always start the relationship in the lead role and never following.

How to please her

In order to please a black woman sexually you must clearly "own it." Without owning it you cannot please her. Despite obvious influences of European fairytales of love and romance as her man, you must possess the ability to cure her curiosity. Though she fancies a storybook romance, believe it when I tell you that she most prefers her man to "own it." He should tame her sexuality with his masculinity because despite all she is still 100% African at heart no matter what shade of brown her skin tone is. She is a complete lioness at heart and her man's back must be strong enough to endure the weight of her passions. We live in a society that places a premium on saying the right or appropriate things or being politically correct, so much so that many women are forced to hide their true desires. Thus, they become sexually inhibited in their ability to express their sexual needs. Many sistas have become less than honest about what they expect sexually from their men. Some have gone as far as to proclaim that size does not matter. A black woman that claims that she does not care if her man has a small penis is either a liar or a deluded idealist who has spent too much time roaming in non- African American circles of friendship. Every black woman wants to be proud of her man's ability to "put it down" or "put it on her" whenever she wants it. However, we are living in a day and time where many sistas start to make deals with "suspect men" who are not up-to-par in the department of lovemaking. Many men come up short and are not prepared to lead a relationship. This is causing major problems in black relationships leading to mass confusion among black women about what a

"Real" man is. This confusion has led some sistas into the arms of other women through a lifestyle of bisexuality or straight up lesbianism. The recent rise in bisexual experimentation among black women who would otherwise live their lives as "straight" heterosexual females has an explanation. It is a direct result of a lack of suitable black men, who are able to lead a romantic relationship with a woman. Therefore, what does she want from you? How can you please her? I'll put it this way... A black woman understands what her man covets most. She knows the things in his life he places value on, whether it is his mother, car, art, hobby etc. She will often compare her worth to these things in order to see where she stands in her man's life.

To my sons:

She watches how you obsess over your favorite car. She observes how you wash and wax every inch of it until you see your reflection in your hard work. She wants to be your masterpiece. She desires for you to see your reflection in her eyes for they are the windows to her soul. She never fails to notice how carefully and firmly you glide your hands across every inch and curve of your favorite set of 24 inch rims. She wants you to notice her curves as well. She notices how firm, yet careful you are and not timid or shy about handling your favorite things. She wants to be your favorite girl. She realizes that you own your car therefore; she wants you to own her "it." Own what? Her spot of course. The spot only the right man in her life can ever come to know and take ownership of. You see that spot is her sexual real estate. It is the space in her life that makes her want to let go, where she feels free to give in, scream, or maybe even cry. You see a man that can own her "spot" can be forgiven for nearly any shortcoming. She will gladly endure 9 months of labor and stress and have as many babies as this King can support all because he owns her spot. She may have rented it out to a lesser man at one time or another but don't be faded by that. (A woman will come to you only as perfect as you are) Maybe she leased it with an option to buy but has had a hard time finding a serious buyer because only a "real" man can meet her terms. You would be surprised at the number of black women who
are in relationships or married yet still "renting" out her spot to someone who was never qualified to own it in the first place. A black woman's sexual real estate is

indeed expensive but "owning it" is the only true way to please her.

Getting punked

A passive man about to lose his woman will end up doing nearly anything to hold on to her. Men such as this will end up begging to go down on his lady just to keep her interested.

For many years, black men would never "go down" on a woman or they would not openly admit to it in the presence of their friends. Back in the day "eating-out" was considered "soft" or "weak." Nowadays, men are dropping to their knees like flies before they even say hello to a woman. I mean, seriously, brothas are spitting game to females like; "hey baby, I just want to lick it for you" and the wild part about it is that women are actually falling for it. First, any man that would offer oral sex in exchange for attention is a fool because he obviously does not realize that he has just played himself in her eyes from the start. Now, most women who actually want a man to give her oral pleasure will not instantly give him the cold shoulder because at the very least he got her attention and stimulated her curiosity with his bold proposition. It is no different than a woman walking up to strange dude up in the club and saying; "can I give you head?" Most men would find themselves imagining the possibilities of such a proposition. Women are the same, except a black woman will lose respect for a man in a minute once she figures out that she can get him to "bite the coochie" before she even decides to be with him or not. You see, black women are severely schizophrenic when it comes to this issue. On the one hand, they want to see their men as strong and will "dis" and run over a brotha in a second once he shows the slightest sign of weakness. On the other hand they want see him "soften up" just a little bit by orally pleasing her from time to time. Here is a testimonial from a woman named Latosha:

I remember going to the club one night and meeting this guy at the bar. I thought he was a little cute, so I gave him some conversation. He paid for my drinks and we socialized. We went out to the dance floor and danced. He kept trying to whisper something in my ear but the music was too loud so I kept asking him to repeat himself. Finally, I heard him ask if he could "eat me." I was like damn! By then I had a couple of drinks, so I was like, 'are you serious?' and he was like 'hell yeah, I am serious', so we ended up leaving the club and going to his car in the parking lot. I did not have to kiss this guy or anything all he wanted to do was go down on me so I let him. I mean it felt really good. I came and everything. So, after he was finished he was like, "can I call you" at first I wanted to ask him; 'are you serious? ', but I could tell he was dead serious so I was like, "yeah" and so I gave him my telephone number. This nigga calls me every day and all I do is avoid his phone calls. I mean he knew what he was doing when he went down on me and it did feel good but for some reason I just don't want to holla at him like that.

To be quite honest a black man cannot win when it comes to performing oral sex on a black woman because if he does not do it she will accuse him of being overly macho and inattentive to her sexual needs. If he does do do "it," she will eventually become disinterested as a whole and consequently lose respect for him. Many men get a kick out of watching their woman climb the walls during oral sex. However, if she starts to tell you every now and then that she has a headache whenever you want regular sex, but will somehow always manage to find the strength to turnover and part her legs just so you can eat her out, chances are you are "being played." She has lost total interest in your penis and now all she wants you to do orally please her. You see men have gotten things backwards. Some men actually believe that when they are "going down" on a woman they control her sexuality when in reality she is the one in control because she has you on your knees, penis dry as sandpaper, giving her pleasure. Now I am not saying that all men need to stop performing oral sex. (to each his own). What I am saying is that some things are so critical to how you are perceived in the beginning stages of your relationship with a black woman, that it would be a wise thing to allow the relationship to mature before exploring premature sexual activities. Such actions may bring your "manhood" into question. Once a black woman convinces herself that her man is weak and only good for giving her oral pleasure, she has in effect "taken" his manhood. Thus, he can never retrieve his "manhood status" back from her. You see a woman may not have the power to make a man a man, but she definitely has the power to confirm his manhood by either acknowledging it or denying it.

Who is on top?

During sex, a woman who exemplifies innate "Queen B" qualities will usually be the one in control of the sexual activity. By this I mean, she usually attempts to dictate the when, the where, and the how, when it comes to the act of having sex during the relationship. "B's" usually like to ration out sex to their men in order to control them. Often sex with this kind of woman resembles a negotiation more than a spontaneous occurrence. In short, she will use her sex as a weapon in order to tame her man into submission. One of the "Queen B's" sexual goals is to make you feel like she has done you a favor when and if she decides to give up the "goodies." However long it may take, the true Queen B will ultimately get to this point because her true desire is not to serve but to be "equal" with or outright lead you. This is why in the end a woman like this who desires to start a family will choose a man who has a passive nature, one whom she can manipulate and dictate the terms and tempo of the relationship. The downside of this is that a Queen B married to a non-alpha passive man will usually end up screwing other men on the side. The reason for this downside is that she did not marry her husband because she respected him. Instead, she married him because he was a convenient fit to her dominate personality, and she needed him to participate in her version of a family that is not necessarily headed by a man.

In essence, she chose a pawn instead of a King. A King holds authority over the kingdom (marriage). The pawn is simply expendable and used for whatever purpose. Because of this dynamic, the Queen B is far more likely to find sexual pleasures outside of her marriage. In order to keep this woman faithful she must first respect her man. Any woman that does not respect her man will be disloyal to him. If she decides to cheat, she will usually do so with a man who is an Omega Male with a much more clever personality than her mild mannered passive husband'. The reason for this is that every "straight" woman, especially a "Queen B" is turned on by the illusion of controlling two relationships. She is aroused and fascinated by the Omega's sly nature and antisocial way. However, this sexual attraction does not automatically translate into submission by these types of women. Black women who have not been groomed for marriage and are natural "Queen B's" find difficulty submitting to the male sly nature of these kinds of men because it conflicts with their aggressive personalities.

Hoe

What is a Hoe exactly? This is a word commonly used in the streets to describe a female that virtually every guy in the neighborhood has had a piece of. She is a woman with a reputation for being "easy" or indiscriminate in areas concerning sexual relations with men. Oftentimes, there is a plethora of meanings for the word hoe, however, they are related based on the idea that a woman that is labeled a hoe is somehow less than other women.

As simple as these definitions may appear in truth a hoe is a lot more complex and diverse than these simple descriptions imply. First, most if not all women have a little bit of "hoe" in them. By this, I mean that most women enjoy sex just as much as men do. They just approach it slightly differently for fear of bringing their virtue and character into question. You see, most men do not mind a woman with a little hoe in them. However, women often become stigmatized with the "hoe" title when their sexual exploits become public knowledge among their peers. Most individuals attain a particular social reputation either in high school, college, church, or the work place. In these social environments people are often closely knitted together in peer groups where they are judged according to the common knowledge that has been made public about them. Women who jump from boyfriend to boyfriend within the same social circles often will attain the initial reputation for being "easy." "Easy" means that she makes herself easily available to men when it comes to forming intimate relationships with them. However, she attains the title of a full-blown "Hoe" in two ways. The first way is by the mouths of other women who are obviously jealous of her ability to grab the attention of the men around with ease. Jealous women will often spread the "she's a hoe" rumor in order to assassinate the suspect's character in the eyes of men in the peer group. By doing this, they are able to control or eliminate some of the fierce competition for male attention. The second way women attain the title of "hoe" is by having sex with men who kiss and tell.

Buddy's big mouth

I remember when I was in high school a few of the guys, including myself would gather outside of the basketball gym during breaks and watch the girl's basketball team practice. We would be in our own little conversations down on the south side of the gym near the double-doors just kicking it waiting to go home. This one particular day we were checking out the girls on the basketball team. We would talk about each one and how "fine" she was. Well, eventually "Buddy" who was in a serious steady dating relationship with one of the girls on the team started talking about how freaky she was and how she always wanted to have sex and how well she would "go down" on him and so on. He went on and on about every detail of their sexual relationship in front of us. Meanwhile, she was running up and down the court looking back at him innocently, smiling at him never knowing that he was running her reputation straight to hell in front of us. Afterwards, all the guys in the locker room could talk about was how messed up it was for him to put his girl's business in the street and how shocking it was to know that she was that "freaky". Nevertheless, their relationship ended after high school and I ended up going to the same university as she did and we shared a class together. By then, I thought that she was kind of pretty and I think that she started to show a little interest in me as well. However, his vivid description of their sexual exploits both intrigued and repelled me simultaneously.

A woman who is a lady in the church and a hoe in the bedroom is not a bad deal at all. As a matter of fact, it is an ideal held by most men when it comes to how they would prefer their woman to act behind closed doors. The problem usually arises when her sexual appetites, skills, and talents are made public either by her own carelessness or by the betrayal of her immature lover.

Understanding her mind

A Hoe's sexual behavior is rooted in her childhood. Hoes, in general, tend to use sex for love and attention. The Hoe usually grows up in a neglectful, emotionally starved home. Eventually, sex becomes a replacement for lack of attention, emotional support, and as a means of escaping boredom. This behavior becomes the way she obtains peace of mind. It is her major coping drug for the stresses of everyday life. A Hoe's sexual behavior is less about sex, and more about the search for that elusive thing called love. Sex just happens to be the means that a Hoe uses to find what she is looking for.

A common myth or misconception associated with "Hoes" is that they are prostitutes or just plain "loose" women. This is not true at all because a prostitute is actually a "Queen B" with a financial plan. A "B" that has fallen down on her luck in life usually will turn to prostitution to pay the bills, simply because she has no other alternative. Her body becomes her means of survival and a way to maintain control over her sexuality; she views men as "tricks" because she plays them for money. A Hoe could never survive in this kind of world because her entire idea of sexuality is drastically different from the Queen B. It takes a true "B" to survive in the streets long enough to make money selling her body. You see a desperate "B" in a bad situation will always use her body to get what she wants out of life.

A Hoe's reasoning for giving up sex is entirely different. First off, men do not have to pay to have sex with a Hoe because she is not using her body to survive and make money. She is using her body to feel necessary and to feel a sense of purpose. The Hoe figures that if this is what guys want from her, then this must be the sum of her entire worth and value. Therefore, she assumes that "giving it up" is something that she is supposed to do in order to be accepted by men.

Everyone remembers that one girl in the neighborhood who was "easy." She would give it up to every dude in the neighborhood. She was everybody's girlfriend eventually. Ironically, these women make both Queen B's and Wives extremely nervous and insecure because the Hoe has such an easy and passive nature. Now, when I say that a hoe has an easy and passive nature, I am not implying that all Hoes are easy-going people. What I am saying is that they have an easy and passive sexual nature, especially when it comes to relating to men. A unique quality that Hoes have is the ability to make men feel at ease and secure in their presence. A Hoe really knows how to make a man feel like a man because sex is second nature to her. It is her talent or gift. A hoe will communicate to a man with her body or with words how great he is, and how strong and satisfying he is to her. A Hoe will make a man feel like he has conquered the universe when she is making love to him. She can do all these things without effort because in reality she is not trying to play him she is trying to win his approval and affection. Therefore, it is her mission to support his fragile male ego by complimenting his masculinity with her powerful femininity. The Hoe aims to please, no doubt. A Hoe will do things to a man sexually that most wives simply cannot do and most Queen B's are too proud to do. The Hoe finds her absolute purpose in pleasing her man so there is nothing that she will not do to both please and keep him. Of all the four kinds of women, the Hoe has the most powerful feminine energy. It is this woman that throughout human history has brought kings, prophets, and kingdoms to their knees. Another characteristic of Hoes is that they do not have to be stereotypically "pretty." Many Hoes are in fact, very beautiful and pleasing to the eye, but this is not what always attracts men to them. Hoes have an extremely powerful sexual energy that is almost irresistible to most men. When she walks into the room, all the other women grab and clutch their men very tightly. She is by nature a showstopper one who demands attention by virtue of her presence and magnetism. Men gravitate to her because of her easy and approachable nature first, and then her sexual energy keeps them very much hooked and interested. A man has to do very little if any hardcore "mackin" to pull this type of woman because she is already glad to see that he is into her. It gives her a sense of self-worth just to know that he is interested. Unfortunately, this easy-going side of the Hoe often leads her into trouble when it comes to men. She often indiscriminately allows any and every kind of dude into her space. She is especially prone to being victimized by Beta men or Players. These men often find the most physically attractive women, who may happen to be Hoes, and destroy them emotionally, physically, and spiritually. Beta men are driven by an inferiority complex that often causes them to use the Hoe to reaffirm their manhood through the sexual conquest of her mind and body. This often leads to emotional abuse, multiple pregnancies, and even HIV infection. These men often reduce Hoes to a feeling of "nothingness" after they are done with them. If a Hoe should have to choose between the lesser of two evils, then she should choose to be with an Alpha male type man rather than a Beta because of the "controlling" nature of the Alpha. You see, the Alpha man's need to control or manage other people is sort of a balance for her. He will not tolerate infidelity from her. Instead, he will seek to change and control her sexual habits to best suit him. In other words, the Alpha will try to channel the Hoe's focus on him and nowhere else. Now, the downside to this is that domestic abuse is not far behind this scenario, especially if she is a naturally stubborn individual. Most Hoes generally have a long list of past lovers who still call her off-and-on whenever the mood strikes them. In an Alpha/Hoe relationship, this can cause a great deal of stress and aggravation. The Alpha will spend most of his time fighting off her old flames because of his need to control his environment. However, if she has a passive nature the two may surprisingly balance each other because her desire to follow goes hand in hand with the Alpha male's need to lead.

In comparison to the Hoe, a Queen B by nature can be unreasonable and bull-headed. A Wife may or may not possess an easy-going nature, but both the Queen B and the Wife share a common clear disdain for the Hoe because they perceive her as a very real threat. This is because married and single men alike are quite vulnerable and taken by the "easy" nature and submissive sexual energy of the Hoe.

A question of virginity

Finding a virgin in today's society is so rare that most men automatically assume that all women have some kind of sexual experience. Some believe that virginity is the key to finding a good woman, as if it some type of assurance against the possibility of a woman being a hoe. In today's society all physical virginity means is that the female has not had the opportunity to have sex. There is very little, if any moral virtue attached to the idea of virginity. However, if a man finds a woman who is a physical virgin, then his next order of business is to find out how many men she has performed oral sex on while trying to maintain the sanctity of her vagina. As outrageous as this may sound, it is definitely something men should consider. This is because many women claim physical virginity but their minds are all screwed up.

Some women, who claim to be virgins, have done everything under the sun, except allow a penis to penetrate the walls of her vagina. Therefore, virginity may just be a physical reality but may not mean anything in areas of morality and good sexual character. A man should not choose a woman simply based on something as trivial as virginity, instead he should choose a woman who has a solid reputation in each of the four social environments that I mentioned earlier: high school, college, church and the work place. If a man finds a woman who has a solid reputation in at least a couple of these arenas, this can indicate a woman who has made a conscious effort to carry herself with self-respect and a form of sexual dignity. Still, the highest form of respect granted to a woman is when the men that she has had past relationships with will not put her sexual information out on "Front Street" after their relationship is over. If a man refuses to discuss his sexual relationship with an ex-girlfriend to others, this is a clear indication that she is a woman worth having.

Marry her?

One of the main drawbacks of a Hoe is that they are prone to cheating on their men. A Hoe will usually allow another man to sex her down whether she is involved in a serious relationship or not. You see, there are at least two types of Hoes. The first type is the basic "run around screwing any and everybody" type of Hoe. The second type is the kind of hoe that needs to be in a relationship to do her dirt. These are "undercover Hoes." Many of these kinds of women usually will form meaningful relationships with each sex partner, in order to legitimize the act of having sex with them. Undercover Hoes have a pattern of forming these love relationships, which often includes boyfriend-girlfriend unions and even marriage with the men that they meet. Sex with these men is all part of a deal Hoes make in exchange for love and secrecy. Despite these "major" relationships, these women usually have many different sex partners whom they visualize as close friends or intimate lovers. These encounters usually occur in sequence with each other. Undercover Hoes have an extremely hard time trying to find fulfillment and stability in any of the relationships they form. These women habitually keep returning to former relationships such as old boyfriends, in order to keep the emotional lines of communication open in each relationship.

The undercover Hoe does not believe in burning bridges. However, she will at times randomly create new relationships when she has lost the affections and attention of one of her many ex-lovers. She jumps from man to man trying to find that one relationship that would ultimately bring her peace and completeness, usually she is never quite so lucky to find what she is looking for. Her path in life is shrouded in secrecy and littered with heartache after heartache leaving a trail of tears and self-doubt. Any man who tries to settle down with her is in for a world of hurt and frustration because it will only be a matter of time before she slips up and cheats on him. This is why, at first glance, Hoes do not make good wives at all. Any man thinking about getting involved in a serious relationship with a Hoe needs to think long and hard on the matter because these women often ruin the best of men.

One of the unique things about a Hoe is that deep down she is really looking to give love and to be loved. She also dreams of being swept off her feet and whisked away into the security of marital bliss. Most are not "bad" folks, in fact at least, in their minds; they always have the best of intentions when entering a new relationship. The Hoe sees each new relationship as a new beginning, a fresh starting point, an opportunity to reboot and put her past behind. Unfortunately enough though, most can never truly escape their past because the past is usually what dictates how they treat their future. What I mean by this is that Hoes, through years of practice, develop patterns of sexual behavior that they grow accustomed to.

These patterns are based on easily submitting to each new sex partner without discretion or any form of ethical or moral consciousness. Each sexual endeavor for her is as familiar as a handshake. She is usually aware that her sexual patterns of behavior are not acceptable in a "love" relationship; however, putting an end to this kind of systematic behavior is often easier said than done. This is the sort of baggage that Hoes bring into a relationship, the inability to separate herself from her past. Despite all of this up front information, there is still no shortage of "sucker dudes" out there who are on some "Captain Save-a-Hoe" ego trip that are willing to drag themselves through all kinds of hell and degradation. These types of men are usually well meaning but yet still misguided in their attempts to change his Hoe into a lady. Old school men used to say that if you want to know how to guide a woman then you should always treat a Hoe like a lady and a lady like Hoe. Thus, you will never go wrong in your attempts to get her to be what you want her to be.

Freak

A Freak is a woman who uses the act of sex as a form of recreation or entertainment. She is absolutely devoid of emotional attachment during sex. The Freak "mind-set" is the darkest side of a woman's personality because it is the most self-serving and destructive. What makes the freak different from the "Hoe" is that the Hoe is usually trying to "please" or serve the man she is having sex with. She may or may not derive physical sexual pleasure from the experience. Instead, she feels more of a sense of purpose when she is having sex with him. The Freak, on the other hand, is "in-it" strictly for the physical stimulation and selfish sexual gratification nothing more nothing less. A Freak views sex as a kind of sexual game of "all you can eat" she wants to taste a little bit of everything on the menu.

A Freak is the most untrustworthy of all the classifications of women mentioned in this book. Whenever she cheats on the unlucky man in her life, you better believe that she "meant" to do it. There is no such thing in her mind that would lead her to excuse such behavior as some kind of accident or "oops it just happened." A Freak's mind is like one big sexually charged amusement park and in her world; she ain't leaving until she has experienced every ride in the park. Marriage to this kind of woman should be avoided at all costs because of all the women, she is the most risky proposition for a man on the hunt for a "loyal woman. " The words "faithful" and '"Freak do not even belong in the same sentence because like the "Queen B" she is driven by her selfish nature.

Men on the prowl for sex with no strings attached, need to be especially leery of these types of women. The risk of disease alone should warrant caution. So how does a woman actually become a Freak? Are they born, made or do they simply evolve into freaks? Point blank, most, if not all women, have just a little bit of "freak" in them just as most women have a little Queen B, and Hoe in them as well. However, a true Freak is either born or turned into a Freak via some unique sexual experience. "Turning-out" is the process of turning an otherwise normal woman into a Freak. When a woman has been turned out sexually, she loses most, if not all, of her sexual inhibitions and innocence to the point where a sexual appetite drives her more than her common-sense. I guess a more intellectual term for a Freak would be a "sex-addict."

She cheats

All women at some point and time have contemplated if they would cheat on the men in their lives. However, in the Freak's case, it is never a matter if she will cheat; it is simply "when" she will cheat. The difference between a Hoe that cheats on her man and a Freak that does the same thing is surprisingly different. You see, a Hoe is just as inclined to cheat on her man as any other woman but she usually does it for a whole set of different reasons than does the Freak. The Hoe, despite her hoe-ish behavior, will in fact feel a great sense of remorse and a deep sense of self-loathing while lamenting her sexual indiscretion. However, the Freak feels no sense of remorse because she is not driven by any particular moral codes that would invade her sexual conscience. Any remote sense of remorse that she may feel will stem not from her guilt, but instead it will stem from the fact that she hurt someone else's feelings in the process of gorging herself sexually. The reason being is that most Freaks commit acts of infidelity on purpose with the intent not to hurt anyone's feelings. She wants to please herself sexually with someone she perceives to be different, not necessarily better. Before a Freak gets to the point where she is having sex with another person outside of her relationship she has already surveyed the opportunity in her mind a couple of times over. This is all before she actually gets down to the business of screwing the guy. In direct contrast a Hoe will (at least in her mind) usually "end-up" cheating on her man. This is due in part to her being caught up in a circumstance where some guy pushes up on her really strong for some sex, thus challenging her already weak will power. With a Hoe there is usually no planning or premeditation involved in sexual infidelity. The circumstance generally dictates the outcome. A Freak on the other hand scans the crowd with her eyes measuring up the potential for a possible sexual rendezvous with a man other than her boyfriend or husband. She is like a child in a candy store the more variety available to her the better. Therefore, all men need to take care and be mindful not to turn their "good-woman" into a Freak. Though the opportunity to do so may be oh, so tempting and inviting, I would urge any man who really does love his woman not to "turn-her out" sexually during their relationship.

I will give you an example; many men fantasize frequently, for one reason or the other, about observing their woman having sex with another woman or having a "threesome." These men derive sexual pleasure just at the thought of this kind of sexual event. However, I would suggest that men who consider this possibility to think long and hard on the matter before actually going through the process of talking their woman into this kind of situation. I say this because a woman who loves her man is usually willing despite her better judgment, to indulge and entertain his sexual fantasies.

The ability to please a man through granting his sexual wishes is a kind of "Jeanie in a bottle" power and quality

75

that most women have. However, men need to take care not to wish for the wrong thing because just as in the Arabian tales of the "Jinn" or Jeanie, often times the man wishing becomes the victim of his own greed and lust. In other words, any man who "wishes" to see his woman engaged in sex with another woman may find out that she may start to enjoy the situation more than he does and end-up preferring the emotional and sexual attention of another woman rather than his.

Corrupting a good woman

Men, who try to turn an otherwise "straight" woman out and into a situation such as this, will usually start by trying to break down her natural objections. He may take her to a local strip club, so that he can use it as an opportunity to get her comfortable in the presence of naked women dancing provocatively. He will introduce this idea as if it were an innocent gesture of good will, a daring thing for them to do together that is a little different and out of the ordinary. Spicing up the relationship may also be an excuse used to make her more comfortable with the whole idea. Most men realize that women have a reasonable amount of curiosity when it comes to what goes on inside of a strip club. Understanding this curiosity, men manipulate it to their advantage. Eventually, most women will go along with the idea just to satisfy her man's fantasy. After she agrees to go with him to the strip club, he buys her a few drinks and starts to observe her every reaction in order to gauge his next move, which of course will be to buy her a table dance. This is where the fun really starts because now he can observe how she reacts to another dancing sexually

sexually in front of her. This is the beginning of a well thought out breakdown process. You see, instead of the guy doing all the work trying to break down his woman's defenses, he uses a third party to assist him, the stripper who is a professional seductress to do the initial work. After the stripper moves into action the boyfriend doesn't care what reaction or response he gets from his lady whether it be shock, shame, embarrassment, blushing, or anger. Either of these responses will yield a great deal of information concerning her receptiveness to the whole idea of having a "threesome." Out of all the responses, blushing, or anger are most preferred when it comes to turning a woman out. If she blushes at the site of a naked female dancing seductively in front of her, it may reveal another sexual side of the girlfriend or wife that she has kept secretly away from the prying eyes of her man. On the other hand, anger is just as good because if a woman gets upset and walks out on a table dance, this may reveal a deep-rooted sexual insecurity that can be exploited later. Nevertheless, this is a common method used by men seeking to turn their women on to the idea of a "threesome."

The Wife

Altogether a good wife is most like a lioness. You see, like the lioness she can be powerful, intelligent, and sexy. The female lioness can go out, hunt all day, bring down prey several times larger than herself, and drag the carcass of her kill several miles back to the den using her great skill and stamina. Once she gets the carcass back to the den she refuses to allow the cubs or even herself to take a bite before the leader of her pride, the male lion takes a bite. Only after the male lion has eaten does she finally indulge herself and appease her hunger. So the question is, how on earth can a lioness being the most feared, productive predator in the jungle go out, take down a huge beast several times stronger and heavier than herself, drag it back to the den and wait for some "lazy" male lion to eat first? Why doesn't she fight him over the meal, why does she submit a meal to the male lion that she worked long and hard to bring down? This is a kind of mystery, but what it reveals is that as powerful and successful as the great lioness is, she still submits herself to her leader. This act of submission creates order and balance keeping the lions as a "collective" group at the top of the food chain at least in the jungle. When a black woman figures out this mystery of the lioness, she will have discovered her true self.

In the minds of most men, the "Wife" status is the highest and most respectable. All men generally want their women to carry themselves with the dignity and regality that most good wives represent. A good Wife can be a serious "Queen B" when it comes to defending her children or she can be a pretty good "Hoe" for her man, giving him sex whenever and wherever he wants it without complaint, morning, noon, and night. Likewise, a good Wife can be her man's biggest "Freak" behind closed doors away from the prying eyes of the public. Therefore, you see a good Wife is a combination of the Queen B, Hoe, and the Freak. The difference is her upbringing and the priority of family.

A woman's power

The Wife is the most coveted category of woman because in this capacity she is able to fulfill her greatest potential as a mother and a companion. The greatest gift that a woman can offer her husband, ironically, is also her greatest sacrifice and that is her "submission." By submitting her will to the husband, she empowers him to succeed, as well as be respected. A man who cannot convince his woman to believe in his vision for life most likely will not be able to convince others to take him seriously. A woman's belief in her man is an almost supernatural force that propels and guides her man to greatness. The invisible energy that she produces sustains him during times of peril and hardships and gives him strength and confidence in order to persevere despite all odds. Only a man's wife or woman can have this type of effect on him. Not even a mother's love can compare to the supernatural faith that a wife has in her husband's ability to do his "thing" and be successful at it. However, the modern black woman sees submission as a form of weakness because she believes that she deserves to be her man's equal. She does not view submission as a power rather she considers the very concept beneath her.

A Wife on the other hand should understand that she is submitting her "force of will" to her husband, thus empowering him to lead the family with a singular vision. By her decrease, the family as a collective unit increases its productivity, sustains longevity, and bonds together as a much stronger cohesive unit. All of her intelligence, gifts, and talents should be presented to her husband to use at his discretion for the well-being of the entire family. A woman's duty to her husband is to help him fulfill his purpose by taking on his way. In other words, everything that he is about she becomes also. This is often referred to as a "ride or die chick," "a down female" or simply a loyal Wife.

Rule #4
There are only 3 kinds of men

Alpha Men
(MACKS)

Beta Men	Omega Men
(PLAYERS)	(SNAKES)

Wolves have a unique and well-defined social system that begins with the dominant males called Alphas. The middle ranking males are Betas and the lower ranking male dogs are called "Omegas."

The Alpha Male (MACK)

Alpha males are the top-ranking men in the African American social group. An alpha male in this group is not stereotypically "handsome." They come in all shapes and sizes and often exude a hyper-masculine energy that attracts women to them. Unlike other ethnic groups where physical male attractiveness is a premium, among black men an over-preoccupation with male beautification is often seen as less than manly and effeminate. Thus, the position of 'Alpha Male' among black men usually describes a man that is hyper-masculine and wields influence over the other males in his social group. Black men who are alphas are usually aggressive, competitive, ambitious, and strong-willed. These men make things happen and have the innate ability to use either physical or mental aggression to get things done. Among African American men there are only two types of alpha males. The first is the "Alpha Don." He is an absolute shot-caller. The name of his game is "control." He must be the authority from which others take their cues. The "Alpha Don" is not necessarily "book smart" but "street smarts" serve him just as well when it comes to him getting what he wants. Most Alpha Dons start out as hustlers, in the black community. The hustler is that individual who is self-motivated to achieve his goals by his own means, without working a "straight" gig or job. However, there are plenty of "po-hustlers" out there. This means that they may be hustlin to make money, but for whatever reason, they are unable to upgrade their hustle by delegating the footwork to others. This reflects a lack of ability to manage other people, which is one of the key characteristics of an alpha male, period. Black men who are Alpha Dons can have little or no education. However, they still end up doing major business in arenas populated by individuals who are more educated. Even though less educated, they may have just as much or more money and opportunity as well. The Alpha Don has "magnetism." He attracts people who tend to need direction in their lives and he is always more than happy to oblige them, so long as they are willing to submit to him without question.

The second type of African American male alpha would be the "Alpha Supreme." Alpha Supremes are usually highly educated with high IQs. These men are mostly "self-taught" masters and traditional education is boring to them. Ultimately, their achievements are studied as college courses. They are charismatic, idealistic, stubborn and innovative. These men have a knack for figuring people out and getting them to do their bidding. Manipulation is this alpha's weapon of choice. He is more mentally aggressive than anything else because he is fully aware that most men in his circle cannot out-think him. He does not view subordinate males as simply "worker bees" but instead he would rather see them as "students' of his. Alpha Supremes are the creators and innovators of their group. People follow them because they seem to have the ability make something out of nothing. An Alpha Supreme inspires those around him and this is his ultimate method of control over them. Now for the record, alpha male behavior among black men often overlaps both of these types. However, most alpha black men usually display one of these two types more dominantly than the other.

The Mack

An alpha black man in a dysfunctional form is a "MACK." Mack is a word that originated in the streets back in the early 70's. It usually described a man who was a "Pimp." Later on, it became a word used to describe any man who could control a woman by using mental or physical aggression. In some circles, this kind of man is a "womanizer" or lady's man. A true Mack did not have to prove his manhood to a woman. Instead, he would flip the script on a female by putting her in a position where she felt as if she needed to prove herself to him. This man did not purchase cars and clothes hoping to attract women. Instead, he found women who were willing to buy him these kinds of gifts and lavish him with attention. A true Mack could be penniless and still manage to attract a top-notch woman. A typical Mack is a man who outwardly appears to be ordinary or unpolished yet has an extremely beautiful, intelligent woman hounding him. She hounds him, even though outwardly she appears as if she could do much better and have any man she wants. The reason for this is because, it is not his material possessions, or lack thereof, that attract women to him. It is his "mind," that attracts women. Macks are attractive because of their ability to control others, especially other men. This form of mental manipulation comes natural to true Macks because they were born alpha males in the first place. You see, no matter what, all humans are mammals. All mammals have instincts, and a woman's natural instinct is to get with the strongest male in the group. This instinct will increase her chances of giving birth to strong children who will be able to survive in the world. The first law of nature governs this instinct in a

84

a woman and that law is "self-preservation."

There is actually no real difference between alpha males and Macks except the influence of environment. You see a Mack's environment is usually hostile, violent, and economically poor. A Mack is usually born into a single-parent household headed, primarily, by a woman. These forces are the primary reasons for his dysfunctionality and cause his journey into manhood to be much more difficult than alpha males born into privileged circumstances. As a result, these Macks often take up illegal occupations that are not merely exclusive to womanizing or pimping. Because the Mack is in fact an alpha male, his need to control his environment and those around him often makes him a perfect candidate for high-ranking street positions. They often gravitate to offices such as Gang Leaders and major Drug Kingpins, unless by some chance he is an athlete or has some other opportunity to utilize his alpha male traits in a more productive manner. The problem with a woman forming a romantic relationship with a Mack is that his innate need to be "controlling" often dictates his moods and domestic violence is almost always a part of this equation. Now this is not to say that all Macks are inherently violent towards women. Depending on what kind of woman he is dealing with, physical aggression may often be the result of any rebelliousness on her behalf. Macks are not prone to be hopeless romantics or suckers available to falling in love easily. In their world, these emotions tend to make one irrational and out of control, which is contrary to their very nature. Fatherless from birth, this can often be a death sentence for most Macks because their aggression goes unchecked. These men always seem to learn about consequences the hard way. Challenging authority often leads them into legal troubles, which often lands them in prison. A Mack needs a father or authority figure early on in life. This is so he will learn early what it means to lead by first becoming the follower of his father.

Beta Men (Players)

I remember when I was in the sixth grade the older boys would talk about using a substance called "Spanish fly." Spanish fly was used to get a girl in the mood for sex. Spanish fly was supposed to make girls "hot" to the point where they would practically screw any dude in sight to appease their sexual desires. This was a popular urban legend among pubescent young boys just embarking on adolescence at the time. This was the first time I remember boys actually contemplating or plotting to use a foreign substance to "trick" a girl into having sex against her will. At that point in my young life the concept of having sex with a girl was a very complex proposition not to mention just getting a girl to like you enough to give you a kiss. It was not until I got older that I realized that I had been introduced to the Beta male side of thinking when it comes to getting female sexual attention. As I got older, I began to understand the differences between men who utilized trickery to entice a woman into the bedroom versus those who are invited into a woman's bed. Beta men play these kinds of games in order to undermine or circumvent the will of a particular female who is unsure about the prospect of having sex with them. These kinds of men come in all shapes and sizes; therefore, it can be difficult for most women to distinguish them from others.

What is a Beta Man or Player?

The term "Beta Man" describes a man or select group of men who are driven by the need to prove themselves at nearly every level. This need to prove oneself is fueled by a deep- rooted inferiority complex. A Beta man or Player tries hard to promote an exaggerated persona in order to cover up his lack of substance or character. Men, such as these, tend to spend inordinate amounts of time and money plotting and scheming up ideas on how to impress a woman. Now once again, using the example of the wolf pack, Players are not "Alpha-males" they are not the leaders of the pack however, they are usually stereotypically handsome and take great pride in their appearance. The difference between Beta men and Alpha men is that Alpha men are not driven by the need to prove anything when it comes to gaining the interest of a woman. He is not prone to feelings of insecurity or inferiority. Women are simply attracted to his strength, dominance, and leadership over other males. Having said this, Players are not "Omega men" either, meaning the "outcast" males who reside on the outside of the pack constantly chased away by the other more dominant males. Players would be those men who reside somewhere within the middle of the pack pecking order. These types of men constantly try to gain the attention of the females in the group by doing all

87

sorts of things to impress them. Beta men are not natural born leaders so they spend a lifetime trying hard to prove that the females in the group should recognize them. This inherent insecurity complex is what defines the true nature of the so-called "Player" and it drives much of his thinking process. Beta men or Players seek self empowerment in order to appease their insecurities. They are preoccupied to the point of obsession with gaining materialistic things such as cars, clothes, and status in order to attract a woman and acceptance among their peers.

However, what makes the Player truly different is the fact that he is never truly able to sustain a productive relationship with a woman. This is because throughout the relationship his feelings of insecurity play a major role. A Player's worst nightmare is to be exposed. He does not want women to know that he is unsure of himself. In order to protect himself from being exposed the Player will play the "love game" up to a certain point. The point could vary depending on the situation. A player with a sexual insecurity, real or imagined, will continue a relationship all the way up until the point where he realizes that he has one shot to "hit it." These kinds of men insist on having sex with the lights off. In such case the Player will abruptly end the relationship before any verdict can come back concerning his sexual potency. This behavior prevents him from being embarrassed or exposed by a less than satisfactory assessment from the woman. In direct contrast, Alpha men often desire to have sex with the lights on. Not that he is admiring his sexual prowess. Instead, he must witness the absolute submission of his woman while he is having sex with her. He doesn't close his eyes for a second because he wants to take in the total visual experience. He watches patiently for her to grit her teeth in ecstasy. As her eyes close and roll upwards, her moans and groans inspire him to perform and validate his temporary dominance over her body at that moment. As pleasurable as these situations can be, he could never have sex with the lights off. He is too arrogantly confident.

The Beta man may own a nice ride and wear nice clothes, yet still live at home with his parents. A Player in this circumstance will conduct his relationships with women exclusively outside of the parameters of the home life he shares with his parents, so that he can keep up the appearance of independence and self-sufficiency. However, before the relationship has the chance to deepen, the Player will once again end the relationship abruptly. He has to do this before the woman can figure out that spending so much time with her at the hotel or her place is due to the fact that his parents' home is off-limits.

Many self-proclaimed Players admit openly that the reason why they choose not to settle down is that they want to continue to "play the field." They do not have time for anything serious, when in reality the reason is simple; they fear criticism for not having their act together. Men who devise calculated ways to get sex are Beta males or Players. At times makes it is hard for most women to detect them at first glance. Strangely enough though, as hard as it may be for the average woman to detect this type of man, the average man can spot these types a mile away with no problem at all. The problem is that most women choose to swing solo in their pursuit of companionship. Asking for male advice or input could help guide their decision making process and yield results that are more productive. Men that could help a woman with companionship decisions are usually fathers, brothers, uncles, and male cousins. Most of the time women get caught up in a bad relationship with a guy because she usually has little or no "real" understanding of just how men think and reason.

This lack of understanding, depending on the situation, can cost a woman her reputation, emotional peace of mind, and even her life. Frankly, any father's daughter can end up with a Player, especially if she has not been properly "schooled" correctly by the men in her life that care about her well being. Regardless of the social forces in society that compel women to see themselves outside of the influence of men, all women need guidance from a man. Whether a woman admits this fact or not is insignificant because all women are hardwired by nature to be influenced by men. Players take advantage of this natural tendency and manipulate it to their advantage by using a woman's lack of knowledge and natural instincts against her in order to break her will and gain access to her body.

Player Prototype

Men who fit into the description of the Beta male or the Player are individuals who brag on themselves on a regular basis usually concerning their sexual exploits and conquests real or imagined. Every man has at least one friend in his circle of friends that is always talking about all the women that he has "conquered" at one time or another. Every time you see this dude he always has some new story to tell about the last woman he managed to coax out of her underwear. The stories these guys tell seem to have no end. Such tales are always flavored with the spice of his ultimate conquest of the woman's body. Players are usually the ones in the club constantly pulling on the arms of unsuspecting women whistling and gesturing trying desperately to be noticed. In contrast, Alpha men are least likely to approach a woman in a club because he views this as a situation that he cannot "control." Instead, he would prefer a woman step to him. Many women misinterpret this as "shyness" or a lack of confidence when in fact it is the exact opposite. Unless an Alpha Man receives some "strong," inviting signals from a woman letting him know that it is ok for him to approach her; most Alphas will not bother with the situation.

At first glance, Beta men may appear to be full of confidence, hollering with impunity at any chick that walks by but woe to the woman that rejects his advances. Players are usually sensitive and abhor rejection of any kind. Many of these men will call a woman a bitch in a minute if she rejects his attempts to get her attention. This kind of outburst is a typical Player trait; however, women should learn to spot these aggressive types early. A man who would curse a woman out in public, just because she won't holla back at him surely wouldn't have any problem punching that woman in the face behind closed doors for not giving up the booty.

Bringing your boys a bone

Bragging is never enough for a true Player, though. He is almost border-lined obsessed with proving to his boys that he has had sex with a woman. This type of man is so anxious for acceptance among his peers that proving his manhood through sexual conquest is paramount. Many times this need for a Player to show his boys how much of a Player he is, will result in men who videotape their sexual exploits with women as a form of physical proof. However, providing proof does not stop here. The ultimate proof is always in the amount of influence he has over the woman whom he has conquered sexually.

I remember when I was freshmen in college a few friends and myself were attending a private party where a lot of students from different schools had come to celebrate homecoming. I recall seeing this beautiful young woman standing with a guy who appeared to be her boyfriend. She caught my eye because she seemed a bit out of place and uncomfortable. She was bobbing her head to the music and all, but there was still something different about her. She seemed to not fit in. Despite being in the company of her boyfriend I noticed how many of the guys at the party were gravitating towards her admiring her attractiveness. The funny thing was that her "man" did not appear bothered at all by the attention his friends were bestowing on his girl. He had this half grin on his face and almost seemed flattered and giddy about it. His boys sipped on their buds and slapped him dap every now and then, all the while sizing up their homeboy's girlfriend as though she was a slab of meat. It did not take long to realize that something was up. That something was that he brought his girl to the party to show her off to his friends so that they would admire his good taste. In the process, either he volunteered her to his boys or they demanded to take her for a spin. In either case his girl looked bewildered like she kind of thought something wasn't right, but maybe they were just being really nice to her. So, she smiled off and on while her eyes darted around the room looking for an excuse to breakaway. Nevertheless, it was too late. Her boyfriend, trying to earn his Player card was setting her up to have a "train" ran on her.

One of his boys pulled him to the side, threw his arm around his tiny neck, mumbled something in his ear, and let him go back to his girl. With a signal all the guys retreated to the rest of the party while he prepared his girl for the "train". The aspiring Player broke out some weed and started smoking it he then offered his girl some and she took a few puffs and started coughing and choking. This chick was a "square" trying hard to be down in a party full of strangers, not realizing how her night was about to turn out. After a few more hits on her man's blunt and some beer, she started laughing and giggling aloud. All the while, I could see his boys sitting off in the cut looking serious and focused like vultures waiting for a famished buffalo to stop staggering and fall so they can swoop in and devour the carcass. These guys were going to let her have it once she got good and delirious. Nevertheless, while I went on with my business of having a good time at the party, I noticed the boyfriend taking his girl up the stairs with three of his friends following close behind. This "wanna-be's" intention was to allow his boys to "gang-bang" his girl in the hopes of gaining acceptance as an equal within their group. In his mind, he and his "boys" would be able to all sit around, talk about the shared experience of screwing his woman, and maybe even compare notes. The "wanna be," through orchestrating this act believed that he had won the trust of his "friends." In his mind they would no longer doubt his word. He now had witnesses to his sexual exploits, individuals who would be able to vouch for him when others doubted his Player qualifications.

Omegas (Snakes)

Omega dogs often avoid the Alpha and Beta male members of the pack and never eat first, which in many cases leaves them, scavenging, or stealing the dominant male's food or scraps. Omega dogs travel outside of the pack and are not welcomed among the dominant males. They are not permitted to try and mate with alpha females, either. If the Omega dog tries to mate with the alpha female, the dominant males will usually attack him.

Omegas and Infidelity

Infidelity usually has an extremely negative, if not devastating effect on most marriages, no matter what race you are. However, adultery among African Americans can be a near fatal blow to their relationships because the institution of marriage among blacks is so fragile. This is why adultery has a much more lethal effect on black relationships than most other ethnic groups.

The stresses and struggles of just staying together and beating the odds, often leave very little room for the intrusion of infidelity. There is so much more to lose in an African American marriage because of the constant uphill economic and social struggle to achieve in society in general.

The family is one of the key components of economic development for any group of people because it allows for the immediate transference of wealth. This allows them to become economically mobile from one generation to the next. The disruption of the African American family during slavery has left a lingering economic stain on blacks causing us to remain at the bottom of the food chain in American society. However, infidelity or adultery is an action that sabotages marriages in the black community and wreaks havoc on families that would otherwise be fine without its interference.

In most cases, adultery leads to divorce and messy divorces often leave families not only in shambles, but economically devastated. This is why adultery is a much more volatile issue in the black community. Except in a few cases, most women are not the initiators of extramarital affairs. That dubious title is usually left to the men. Men are more than likely to be the "pursuers" of women, therefore in cases where the women are married this dynamic does not seem to change much. These men are the catalysts of a chain of events in women's lives that ultimately lead to marriages coming to a crashing end. Adultery in the black community is more than a threat. It is venomous and lethal. Men who pursue "legally" married women take on the role of the snake as depicted in the Bible tempting Eve. If men were dogs, then the man who

95

makes seducing married women a practice would be the lower ranking Omega dog of the pack. The process by which a man goes through in order to seduce a married woman is called "snaking" because it requires that one be sly, secretive, and deceptive. When a man has to resort to "snaking" just to get female attention, he demonstrates that he is too cowardly to challenge the husband outright for his woman. He is alternatively inept at getting a single woman to pay attention to him because he is actively "snaking." Dominant men to describe weaker men who sleep with legally married women and run from the consequences use the label "Snake." The Snake is very calculating in his method of operation, when it comes to seducing another man's wife. A true Snake tries to present himself as non-threatening, very friendly, and unobtrusive. The Snake is very artful and experienced in seducing married women. He realizes that there are plenty of lonely, neglected, and horny married wives out there willing to give up some free sex with seemingly no strings attached. The Snake sees this as an irresistible opportunity to get something for nothing. You see the Snake is usually a guy who does not socialize in cliques with other men. He is a "loner" of sorts, and often stands on the fringes of all male social circles. Other men often view the Snake as insignificant, so he goes largely unnoticed. In these circles, traditionally the Snake is not picked in a game of "pick-up basket ball." In a club scene, the Snake finds it hard to compete with other aggressive men for the attention of single females. Therefore, you can usually spot him posted-up in the corner clutching the same drink all night. Now this is not to say that all

Snakes are "nerds." What I am saying is that most Snakes have a hard time bonding and being accepted by other dominant males, thus their ability to capture the attention of a single woman is limited. Single women usually choose men who are at least "one of the guys."

Let's be friends

The first objective is to win the friendship of the married woman. The "he's my friend" status is very important to the Snake because most women protect and defend their friendships, whether they are male or female. This, in turn, creates a portal wherein the Snake can enter the married woman's personal life with a sort of "protected" status. A Snake likes to flatter a married woman with an array of compliments specifically meant to appeal to her vanity. When greeting a married woman in the workplace the Snake uses greetings such as, "hey beautiful" or "how is my girl doing?" A Snake also likes to compliment the married women's choice of clothing with such comments as, "girl you look nice today" or "where are you going all dressed up?" Every time the married woman is in the presence of the Snake, his purpose is to always give her a positive experience. This is so that she will come to cherish, expect, and desire these few but positively delightful flattering comments.

As innocent, as these things may appear on the surface they are actually meant to test the receptiveness of the married woman to infidelity. Once the Snake has gotten the attention of the married woman, and has gained access to her personal life, he then begins to get her to feel comfortable confiding in him about the personal details of her marriage.

The Snake is a great "listener" because he knows that she will have to trust his opinions about her marriage in order to have sex with her. While the husband's ability to listen to his wife is usually divided between the kids, work, and family issues, the Snake can give the wife his undivided attention. However, if the married woman perceives the Snake as pushy, then she will resist his overtures. Therefore, every move he makes, at least in the beginning, is carefully thought out and subtle. At the start the Snake will make a conscious effort to refrain from outright bashing the married woman's husband. He will say things like; "I wish I was your man." or "your husband sure is a lucky guy." The Snake will always let the woman do all the criticizing while ever so subtly instigating her to continue. At times, the Snake will even appear to empathize with her husband in a kind of "we-men can be like that," sort of way. Nevertheless, his main goal is to get the woman to let her guard down. Once he has established a genuine friendship with the married woman, the real hunt begins. The Snake starts to shed the "he's my friend" tag and takes on the more personal role of "honorary girlfriend" status. By taking on this intimate status with the married woman, he gains her ultimate trust. The married woman begins to talk to him freely as though he were one of her close girlfriends, and we all know that women love to discuss relationship issues and problems with their "girlfriends". A Snake that has attached himself to a woman experiencing boredom, restlessness, and or neglect in her marriage is much at ease in her presence because she makes little, if no real demands of him. She is not pressuring him for a commitment of marriage, money, or children because she shares these things with her husband. All she really wants is the never-ending flattery and undivided attention that the sly Snake can most certainly provide.

The second objective of the Snake is to bring the married women to a point where she begins to question every aspect of her marriage. He convinces her to question why she remains with a husband who obviously does not value her opinion, appreciate her unique qualities, pay attention to her ideas, and flatter her endlessly. All women in love usually ignore or hide the imperfections she may notice in her man. If her man has a small business that is making little or no money, she will either ignore it or hide the fact from her parents when they visit. If her man has a little penis, she may not be satisfied but she sure won't tell him that and risk bruising his male ego. If her man has a soft nature or a weak disposition, she will still try to treat him like a man, at least in public. The natural instinct of a woman is to uplift and protect her man. However, if she persuades herself into believing that she can do better or upgrade, then that loyalty usually wanes overtime. After reaching such a point, the married woman begins to pick and question every imperfection that she has come to see in her husband in order to justify and rationalize her newfound feelings for the new man in her life. Eventually, she determines within herself that she feels her husband is taking her for granted. Once a woman thinks her man is taking her for granted, it is downhill from there. She has just given the Snake the "green-light" to start the deconstruction process. Meaning that the Snake will begin to deconstruct and assassinate the character of her husband in order to diminish him further in her eyes. For example, maybe the husband is either unemployed or in-between-jobs and the wife is the primary "bread-winner." This is a common circumstance in modern day marriages. Considering the fluidity of the modern family and the ever-changing U.S. economy, the Snake finds this to be an irresistible target and opportunity to "shine" in the eyes of the unhappily married woman.

We have something in common

The Snake and the wife both work on the same job; therefore, they have "commonality." They share the same career or work environment, which makes them familiar with the other's economic status and income earning potential. The Snake begins to say things like; "how are you going to take crap from a man who can't even pay your bills?" Alternatively, "How is a man who can't put food on the table going to tell you what you can and cannot do?" The Snake's objective at this point in the seduction is to reduce the married women's husband to a dollar figure. The wife slowly begins to buy into these notions. Knowing the employment status of the Snake, she slowly begins to see him as a possible alternative. Even if the husband is the "breadwinner" and makes plenty of money, the Snake will still manage to twist this normally "positive" fact into a negative by harping on how "money isn't everything."

Eventually, he will begin to try and form a "we" or "us" type of bond with the married woman based on the one thing they have in common, their jobs. It is easy for the Snake to accomplish this because the husband sits outside of the wife's workplace. He is not a part of that world and has either limited or no influence over the wife in that particular environment. The Snake takes advantage of this temporary time the wife spends away from her home and family. The Snake starts to casually bring up the topic of his past relationships. He begins to discuss the little things that bothered him about his ex's and how he wishes he could find somebody who had it all together just like the married woman. He talks about how many times he was hurt in the past, and how all he wants in life is to settle down. At this point, the Snake makes it known to the married woman that he is envious of her husband and her marriage, despite her complaints of being unhappily married. He then invites her to give him advice on how to find a good woman who wants to settle down. This technique intends to get the married woman to feel human concern and compassion for his never-ending plight to find true love. The Snake is trying to get the woman to "help" him fix his problem. Men know that women love to try and "fix" them so the Snake uses this female habit against the married woman. The Snake then suggests that the married woman introduce him to one of her "single" friends. This technique is designed to get the married woman actively working on his behalf and thinking about him indirectly on a consistent basis outside of the workplace. However, the more subtle objective is to bring the married woman to a point where she begins to "do the bidding" of the Snake. In other words by using the seemingly innocent request of "hook me up with one of your friends," the Snake achieves his main objective, which is to get another man's wife to "serve" him a personal favor! Now it does not take a genius to see how progressive and aggressive these seemingly innocent personal favors will become as the married woman caters to each one. The Snake wants the wife to think of him outside of work because he knows the more she thinks of him outside of their work environment, the more her desire to want to actually see and be with him will increase. You see, in order to play matchmaker one must actively "think" and ponder on the qualities of the two individual prospects. This is exactly what the Snake wants the wife to do. He wants her actively thinking and pondering about his good qualities, preferably in comparison to her husband's bad ones. He has no real interest in the married women's single girlfriend. He is simply using the girlfriend as a "smoke-screen" in order to get closer to the married wife. As the wife begins to highlight her husband's bad qualities the Snake will start to present himself as a comforter to her. He will let her know that he understands her unhappiness. He starts to give her advice on how things could be better in her marriage if only her husband would be willing to listen and see her side of things. By suggesting that the husband does not understand the wife, the Snake begins the process of alienating the husband, all the while, being careful not to place any particular negative label upon him. The Snake's motive at this juncture of the seduction is to place doubt in the mind of the wife towards her husband. He wants her to start to question whether or not she really even loves the guy. After the seed of doubt has been successfully planted into the mind of the woman, the Snake begins to shed another skin and starts to try and emulate the married women's idea of the perfect man. Everything the woman complains that her husband is not the Snake sheds a skin and therefore, becomes what she desires.

I wanna be your man

For instance, if the wife mentions how the husband doesn't take care of himself physically and is a bit out of shape, the Snake pops up with a free membership for two at the local health and fitness club. He will begin to become more conscious of his outward appearance and will go to great lengths to impress the woman with his style of clothes and attention to hygiene and personal grooming. The Snake will upgrade his wardrobe and dress according to the latest fashions to give him a more youthful image. If the husband never likes to go out to fancy restaurants, the Snake starts to tell the wife fantastic stories of how many wonderful dates to fine restaurants he has taken women. Of course, he mentions how these women did not appreciate his generosity and sense of culture. This technique is simply designed to get her to regret that she is settling for a man who does not recognize how to treat her, while simultaneously getting her to shift her attention away from her husband and into the direction of Mr. Snake.

After he has gotten the woman to thoroughly regret and lament the fact that she married such a bum, she now falls into an emotional stupor. It is at this point that the wife begins to become unsure about nearly every aspect of her marriage. She starts to wonder if things would have been different, if she had met someone else. All the while, the Snake constantly reminds her that he is there if she needs a shoulder to cry on. The Snake now becomes a life raft for a confused and delusional wife drowning in a sea of uncertainty. At this point, he never mentions anything else about her husband. This technique is called "killing the old man." The Snake has spit enough venom on the husband so that the slow poison has taken effect. The wife no longer wants to discuss her family or husband in the presence of the Snake. She almost fears to do so.

This is a sign that the wife now respects her fantasy relationship with the Snake to such a degree that she begins to protect it in her mind against reality! All the while, her "real" husband now assumes a minor or subordinate role to the Snake. The Snake is now the perceived "dominant" male in the mind of the woman. She, now, wants to spend more and more time with the Snake, therefore much of her day is spent daydreaming at her family dinner table contemplating that issue. The married woman now seeks to please the Snake in her appearance, gestures, and ultimately the intimate giving of her body.

Understanding the Snake mind

The Snake has convinced himself that he is in no way responsible for the married woman's decision to betray her husband. He accepts no responsibility for the woman's total disregard for the welfare of her children or marriage vows. He, actually, sees himself as an innocent bystander feeling sorry for the poor "sap" to whom, she is married. The Snake does not consider himself a thief or a "home-wrecker" because he feels that he has made no personal agreements with her husband. Instead, he considers himself a sort of "outside" service provider to vulnerable married women. Thus, the term among the hip-hop community "outside dick" emerged. People within the hip-hop community use this term to describe a man who gets his kicks out of having sex with another man's wife or girlfriend.

The Snake understands the mind of those married women who are willing to seek them out because these men spend an inordinate amount of time fantasizing about women, in general. The Snake makes it his business to know and understand what women really want. For instance, he knows for sure that no matter how happy a woman is in her marriage, she is always glad to know that other men still find her attractive. The Snake is very aware that married women have a plethora of reasons why they would be willing to engage in adulterous affair. He does not underestimate her sense of adventure, nastiness, or sexual aggression. An experienced Snake never wants to meet the married women's family or close friends, especially the husband. You see as long as the Snake does not share any bonds of trust with the married women's family, he feels no sense of responsibility. This is most important when it comes to the husband. The husband is the "wild-card" in this potentially deadly game of masquerade. If the Snake befriends the husband, and the husband finds out about the affair violence in this situation is all too common. The Snake is always aware that his actions could cost him his life, even if the husband perceives him as a total stranger. Many a Snake have been killed or maimed by jealous husbands. As a result, the Snake is very careful not to get too close to the married women's friends, family, or husband. Most Snakes prefer not to organize affairs close to the married women's home. The exception would be instances where the wife has disclosed personal information about her husband, which would make him appear to be a "punk" in the eyes of the Snake. Many black men who are Snakes usually like to get some idea from the married woman of her husband's temperament and physical stature before diving head first into an adulterous affair with her. Most black men, no matter what their economic or social status, don't mind taking it back to the streets when it comes to some other guy trying to creep on their marital situation. No matter what the physical size of the husband, the Snake knows that a hot-tempered husband who is not afraid to pull a trigger is his worst nightmare in this type of situation. This is why the Snake always prefers to err on the side of caution. Many Snakes utilize Internet email and cell phones to coordinate rendezvous with married women. He usually breaks down his victims into groups. The first group of women is the adventurous ones. These women just want to have a good time on the side. These types are easy to conquer because they just want to have little fun. The second group of women is the "neglected ones." They are also easy to conquer because all they really want is a man to tell them how pretty they are. Flattery goes a long way with this group.

The neglected ones desperately need attention from a man, maybe because their husbands are too busy or not attentive. The Snake knows that she will require that he give her emotional support before he will ever be able to hit it. The next group is the "birdies." These women are readily planning to leave their husband and are looking for an upgrade. The Snake usually avoids these types because he is not looking to be her next husband. Another group is the "bored wives." For whatever reason, they have become disenchanted with their marriages and are looking for an outside spark.

Is he playing hard to get?

A major technique used by experienced Snakes is called "catch me if you can." In this game, the Snake tries very hard to appear as though he just wants to be friends with the married women and nothing more. By playing hard to get with her, he provokes her to utilize her own powers of seduction to seduce him. This technique appeals to the woman's competitive spirit. The goal of this technique is to get the woman to take on the personal challenge of seeing if she still has the charm, wit, and sexuality to seduce men. The Snake sits back and allows the woman to use her sexuality to pull him into the affair. This way he knows without a doubt that she is the one doing most of the lobbying. He uses this as back up just in case the stuff hits the fan, and the husband somehow finds out. In a confrontation with her husband, the first thing he is going to want to do is redirect the husband's anger. He will be able to say confidently that the wife sought him out, and that it was her who did most of the lobbying for the affair to take place and ultimately continue.

Once the Snake has gotten the wife "hooked" on trying to seduce him, he will not call her on a regular basis. He will only call on occasions, which are routine enough to show that his still interested. He will want to start touching, but will be disciplined enough to wait until she initiates subtle physical contact. He wants her to feel a tad bit insecure and uncertain about whether or not he is really into her. He begins to make a conscious effort to be unpredictable and offbeat in order to keep the married women's interest in him fresh and renewed. No matter the situation, he will always manage to do the opposite of what she expects him to do, all the while balancing her girlish curiosity with his true intentions.

The Snake knows that the wife is used to everyday routines due to her marital status, therefore he makes a conscious effort to avoid routines. By doing this, the married woman's curiosity is pacified and her boredom is cured. Indirectly, the married woman is pressured into having to prove to herself that she's still got the magic touch when it comes to enticing men other than her husband. This man begins to change the will of the woman by guiding her to a point where she anxiously ignores all of her values and desires nothing more than to be in his presence. Once he has the married woman willing to break her marriage vows and place the welfare of her children in jeopardy, his conquest is almost complete.

If the Snake is not a well-read person he will began to seek out reading materials that will correspond to the married woman's tastes and interests. He does this to pass himself off as a deep thinker, one who concerns himself with the deeper issues of life.

During many of these conversations, he will make every effort to appear to be willing to discuss and own up to his own faults. He will disclose deep -rooted hurts and shortcomings real or imagined in order to appear to be more "open" and honest. He will even go as far as to insist that she ask him random personal questions and promise to be honest in his response, just to gain the opportunity to shine and to win her trust. His words eventually build intimacy with the married woman, whose heart is a fertile ground for his clever words to take root. Ultimately, he pays the married woman the ultimate flattery by explaining to her that she is one of the few people he can talk to about his personal problems. This technique is more effective than actual sex at getting many married women to let down their guard. Once again he will try to create a "we" or "us against the world" theme with the married woman.

The Snake will build these moments up, pieces at a time, until he finally reveals that he truly has feelings for her, but her marriage is an obstacle that makes him feel morally corrupt. He may even go as far as to say that he has never dated a married woman before to add a little authenticity to the deal. After he has thoroughly poured his feelings out, so to speak, he will then convince the woman to admit that her feelings for him are the same. By getting her to admit that she has or is falling for him, the Snake begins to make the fantasy world that they have created on the job that much smaller. It is like being locked in the closet with someone you may or may not be attracted to ordinarily. Eventually, you are going to get down to the business of having sex because you both are sharing the same small, dark, intimate space, and you are seemingly closed off from the rest of the world. This is simple human nature. The Snake with his words tries to make that closet of intimacy between he and the married woman that much darker and closed off.

Now, one must realize that many of the answers given by the Snake to the married wife concerning his personal life will more than likely be false or off-center because he has no intentions of letting this situation come back to haunt him, if it is exposed. A Snake's number one rule is self-preservation. He does not make it a practice of trusting cheating wives with his personal business. For instance, some "rookie" Snakes will allow the cheating wife to come by his crib and have sex with her not realizing that if the situation turns sour her husband will bring all the fury of hell right up to his front door. You see, in the end the married woman will always tell her husband all the information he needs to know about the affair, including personal information about the Snake. She does this because she is eager to prove that she can be loyal to her family despite her indiscretion. Therefore, the Snake's personal information is carved up by the wife and served up as a peace offering to her husband.

The first date

The Snake will eventually initiate the first meeting outside of the workplace or some other environment, when he is totally convinced that he has the woman eating out of his hand. His first suggestion will be something simple like a walk in the park or a visit to the local zoo. These suggestions are purposefully chosen because they are open and public. Such locations make the woman feel at ease with her decision to meet the Snake out in the open.

Finally, he will begin to become more aggressive in his approach by suggesting quick getaways out of town or a rendezvous at the local hotel. The Snake knows that he has been flirting with the woman off and on for some time and has her wrapped up in a non-physical emotional affair of the heart. However, his ultimate goal is to get her to drop her panties and nothing less. Therefore, he makes her begin to feel a sense of obligation to go all the way with it since she has led him on thus far.

After he has convinced her to leave town with him or meet up at a hotel, screwing her is like consummating one's marriage on wedding night. It is just a way to seal the deal. You see the whole affair is a perverted version of her "real" marriage. In a real marriage, one usually "courts" the woman and gains her affections and trust. During infidelity, the Snake also "courts" the married woman to gain her affections and trust. In a real marriage one takes wedding vows, the snake also makes the woman take a vow, a vow of silence and secrecy. Ultimately, in a "real" marriage the union is consummated on the wedding night with sexual intercourse. This tradition also takes place during the married woman's fling with the Snake. He is constantly pushing her to consummate their secret bond by allowing him to have sex with her. The woman inevitably finds herself caught up in two marriages of sorts, catering to both the needs of her husband and the needs of the Snake.

How to deal with the Snake

If you are lucky enough to catch the affair before it actually happens, then your response must be swift and direct. Once your woman begins to mention another man's name in your presence whether he is a co-worker or otherwise, it is your job to sit her down and find out what is going on. In this case, you cannot be a sucker for her obvious attempts to fool you. She may try to ease your mind by harping on how insignificant this individual is. You should always know that no woman frequently mentions another man's name outside of work, if she is not thinking about having sex with him. You must stick to your guns and get to the bottom of that situation.

Now, if your woman tells you outright or in passing that there is a guy at work or anywhere that is trying to holla at her and paying her compliments, there is but one question that you need to ask her and that is; "does he know that you are married?" If she replies "yes." then your conversation with her should be officially over for the moment. You need to find out exactly who this person is what he looks like and confront him immediately. During a confrontation such as this, the best approach is to step to him, as soon as you see him. Do not wait or hesitate go right to him. The perfect situation would be if his back is turned to you, and he cannot see or know that you are even coming for him. This is symbolic of his attempt to get with your woman while your back was turned. If you are not the kind of guy that can handle yourself in a fight, then get your most trusted boys to give you their advice on how best to handle the situation. Remember, the Snake is trying to get something for free. The husband's job is to let him know that there is indeed a hefty price to pay for that kind of brazen trespassing. Now be advised, this type of action is not without consequences. In many cases depending on your timing and location, this could land you in the back seat of a police squad car.

However, any man who will not defend the integrity of his family because he fears a jail cell is not worthy of having a family at all and deserves any fallout that may occur resulting from his woman's indiscretion. Confronting the Snake in this manner sends a defiant message to all parties involved and that message is that; "you will have to go through me to screw my wife!" Often times a mere scuffle on this level will not result in a loss of life or any serious bodily injury.

Though you may be upset at the notion of some stranger overstepping his boundaries into your personal life, it does not compare to the amount of rage and blind fury that most men feel when they find out that their wives have actually slept with another man. Men who resort to violence at this stage of a busted affair are usually highly irrational and temporally unaware of the devastating consequences their anger may produce. These enraged husbands believe that it is their human right to exact deadly revenge on the Snake. Even though it may be his human right, unfortunately for him in this country it is not his "legal" right. If a man is privy to the fact that his wife has been entertaining the notion of having an affair the best thing to do, is step up and meet the situation head on before it goes any further. If that means getting into a physical altercation with the Snake, just to get the point

Across, then so be it. The worst thing a husband can do is to sit back and allow the situation to escalate into a full-blown sexual affair between his wife and another man. Many men will usually have some feeling, notion, dream, or something to alert him to the possibility of his wife's infidelity. He should pay close attention to those instincts early on and take them seriously because they stem from his protective nature.

Who do I deal with first?

Many people argue that it is the woman's responsibility to be faithful to her marriage vows, and that the Snake is an innocent bystander who should not be held responsible for any problems or devastation the infidelity may cause within the woman's family. Contrary to this kind of thinking, the husband should never ignore the Snake's role in the affair by taking his anger out strictly on the wife because this is a most cowardly act. Only after the husband has confronted the Snake should he then go home and deal with his wife, however he sees fit. Some men will choke the hell out of the wife, but do nothing at all to the Snake that has exploited her weakness. Men who exercise this kind of lopsided justice are "punks." If a man is too afraid to deal with the Snake, then he need not say one word to his cheating wife about her indiscretion. He just needs to suck it up and move on without holding the situation over her head.

As stated earlier, the law is seldom on the side of an enraged jealous husband. On the contrary, the law seems to lean more in the favor of the Snake because in the eyes of the law whatever happens between two consenting adults is legal, no matter how much havoc it reeks on the family. According to the law, a Snake has the right to get involved with a married woman so long as she is down for it, regardless. Often times when these outside affairs are exposed, they lead to messy expensive divorces and financially destabilized homes while the Snake simply walks away "scott-free." Who wins in this situation? Well, the wife gets her emotional support and sexual getaway. The Snake gets some free sex, and the husband and the kids get the fallout. In truth, the only winner in the scenario apparently is the Snake, unless of course the husband takes some form of violent action against him. In such cases, the law steps in and protects the Snake by punishing the jealous husband with prison time. What would the police do if a husband actually called them to report a suspicious Snake in their neighborhood scoping out married women? Nothing at all, they would just hang the phone up on him. However, they would send the SWAT team after a husband who takes revenge against a Snake. Snakes do not have to fear any real legal prosecution for getting involved with another man's wife in the kind of society we live in. He can even call the cops on the woman's husband, if the husband even so much as threatens him.

The code never dies

You see, all men have unspoken rules that they live by. These rules maintain a certain level of peace and harmony amongst them. Every man from the time he is old enough to have a girlfriend knows that one of the first unspoken rules of manhood is that you don't pursue a woman who has already chosen a man, no matter what her situation is. A men who violates this rule, willingly breaks the peace and transforms into a Snake among men. The Snake is a snake, not because some attention starved wife has sought him out. Instead, he is a snake because he commits the unnecessary act of sleeping with a married or taken woman. The reason this act is unnecessary is that throughout human history women have always outnumbered men, in many cases as much as thirteen to one. Therefore, there is never a shortage of single women available for men to choose. This makes the Snake's pursuit of married women that much more incomprehensible and unacceptable. The Snake is not a hunter but an opportunist or scavenger, of sorts, roaming the dry desert plains of marriages seeking to nibble on the famished carcasses of confused married women.

Statistics show that nearly 100 million people in this country are affected by extramarital affairs, and of these people, 65 percent of them are married women who are creeping behind their husbands' backs on a regular basis. Back in 1997, Ball State University performed a study that revealed that women under the age of 40 were just as likely to engage in an extramarital affair as men their age. Today, that number is steadily increasing. In today's society, it has become increasingly easier for women to cheat on their husbands. First, we must realize that we are living in an advanced and open society. This is a doubled-edged sword because the more "open" a society is, the more individualistic the people become in that society. Self-gratification and self-expression become priority, thus making it easier for women to cheat on their husbands. Popular culture in America does not view the institution of marriage as important or necessary. We live in a society that attacks the traditional marriage between a man and a woman through the media with images, personalities, and ideas aimed at challenging, if not destroying, the very concept of marriage between a man and a woman.

Nowadays, the majority of women have more of an opportunity to cheat on their husbands. They are working more often outside of the home, alongside men who may start as strangers, but through time and an intimate office setting, slowly become friends. Black women are more likely to get higher education than their male counterparts, so many of them end up staying in school longer earning higher degrees and certificates. All of which leaves them dividing their time between home and career, while sharing the majority of time with male classmates and male co-workers. Therefore, brothas must understand that the moral condition of American society is not necessarily conducive to producing a generation of virtuous women. We are living in a society that is telling our black women through a white feminist agenda, that it is both empowering and liberating to sleep around with whomever, whenever, all in the name of equality. A black man must therefore come to the understanding that given the moral condition of the society in which we live, the chances of his woman seeking out the attention of another man is so high that by default he must assume that his woman may have already betrayed him at some point and time. He must know that some women will risk their marriages, cars, home, kids, and peace of mind, all for some temporary "outside sex."

What women should know about Snakes

A wife who happens to gets involved in a secret relationship with a man outside of her marriage should know that these things are not always as they may appear. Many times, women use excuses to either justify the affair or rationalize it in their minds. By doing this, they are able to continue pursuing the other man with amazingly little or no guilt at all. Such excuses may include the ever so famous; "I deserve to have a good time." Women in this frame of mind often feel unfulfilled and under-appreciated for all their hard work at maintaining the family. In response, they constantly repeat to themselves how they deserve to have a little fun.

Sexual Mind Games

After she has thoroughly convinced herself, that she deserves to have a good time and that all she is doing is having a little fun she starts to move into the next stage. The wife starts to tell herself that no matter what, she is not going to let the flirting get out of hand. She determines that she will control the pace of her little sideline entertainment. Women do this for one reason and one reason only, and that is to start creating a "mental-alibi" or an imaginary witness to her initial motives at the time right before the affair begins. You see no matter how bad things get she never wants her husband to think that she actually meant for it to go down. Now, in order for the husband to believe that it was all a big accident, and his wife's intentions were initially pure, she must first brainwash herself into believing that she was just "flirting for fun." She never meant for the situation to evolve into an all-out affair. You see, all women like to have sex; they just do not like to appear as if they do. The thing most married women do not understand is that they can never really "control" the pace of an extramarital affair because she is the one being played in the first place. Men who seek out married women depend on them to commit themselves willingly to the affair before they start to flex their muscles in the relationship. Up until then, they play the role of counselor, friend, fun-guy etc. These men purposefully appear to be harmless, in order to manipulate a woman into thinking that she has some measure of control in the relationship. These Snakes know exactly how much a married woman stands to lose in the extramarital affair, while they in turn stand to lose virtually nothing at all. You see, according to the Snake there are no real risks involved with kicking it with a married woman. Outside of a remote chance that the husband would be willing to risk going to prison on an assault and battery charge, or worst yet a murder charge, in attempt to exact revenge upon him. Therefore, in his mind, this is highly unlikely, so fooling around with the married woman becomes a win-win proposition. Inevitably, when a married woman steps to an outside male for comfort sexual or otherwise she gives him the power to ruin her. In the mind of the Snake he is thinking; "if this chick is willing to serve up her marriage, kids, reputation, and career to me as some kind of down payment for the opportunity to have sex with me, I must be the man."

Regardless, if the married woman thinks that, her new lover is the sh** or not, by flirting with him, she gives him a tremendous amount of power and leverage over her "real" life. The source of his power over her is "secrecy" the mere fact that she is even talking to him on the side has to be kept a closely guarded secret. Consequently, the Snake is empowered by this secrecy. Every man wants to know a woman's secrets. He wants to know things about her that she is ashamed to tell or show openly. This is why some men seek to "turn women out" sexually because it gives him absolute power over her and brings her to a point of shame. After a man knows a woman's shame, he then assumes an almost complete power and influence over her.

Secret Lovers that's what we are

A married woman screwing around behind her husband's back, usually feels that her deeds are shameful, if not in the eyes of her husband, most definitely in the eyes of her children. She often does not want her co-workers to know about her affair because it can spoil her reputation and ruin her career, so she has to keep the relationship a "secret" from folks at the job. It may appear outwardly that we live in a so-called "progressive" society but issues of moral integrity are ironically still a part of workplace ethical standards. Once a woman's marital indiscretions become public on her job, it could spell disaster for her career. All of this shame and secrecy pushes the Snake into a more dominant role in the relationship, because he is holding all the cards and has the least amount to lose in the situation.

By the very secret nature of this kind of relationship, the wife slowly loses the ability to break the affair off with the Snake on her own terms. Eventually, as the adulterous affair progresses, the Snake will begin to assert more of his will and personal agenda into the relationship. While he is slowly making subtle demands and issuing ultimatums on the married woman, at times she feels torn between catering to the needs of both him and her husband, simultaneously. Eventually, the Snake gets to a point where he starts to believe that he is a better man than her husband. This rationale is usually based on the idea that if the husband was taking care of things at home, then the wife would not be dealing with him on the side. He further becomes increasingly opinionated and possessive when it comes to how much time he is able to spend with her.

One must realize that the Snake is yet still a man, therefore like all men he will grow increasingly jealous when it comes to the married woman receiving attention from other men (including her husband). This sort of jealous behavior, will usually surface wherever the pseudo-relationship began. On the job, the Snake will start to take notice when other male co-workers speak to or show friendly attention to the married woman. Such attention will be tolerated at first, but eventually he will begin to express his displeasure with such attention. This is a sign that the Snake is now starting to see himself as the dominant male in her life, thus having the authority to tell her what she can or cannot do.

The more the married woman adheres to or accommodates these kinds of demands, the more she feeds his ego. As the Snake's ego increases, the more he starts to think, "Man, my game must be really strong, I got another man's woman doing what I tell her to do." When black men play this kind of game it can get serious, because most black snakes are not content with just screwing another man's woman. He desires to take it to another level that is based more so on the idea of "controlling" another man's woman. By controlling another man's woman, a Snake's first move is to get her to give him sex. Secondly, and most important of all he must get her to give him oral sex. This is a form of asserting his manhood on her while getting her to betray her husband completely. The euphoria and sense of power and manliness most snakes feel when they see another man's woman "going down" on them drives them crazy and on to the next level of control.

After he has gotten this woman to screw him and suck him the final act of control is to get her to pay him. Once a married woman starts to dip into her family's finances to purchase clothes and gifts for the Snake, he knows that her marriage is over. It is just a matter of time, and it is at this point that the extramarital affair has reached "the point of no return." The reason I use this reference is that the Snake now has complete control over the relationship and is able to dictate the terms and conditions of the relationship. He may or may not wish to get involved on a more serious level with the married woman. However, in his mind he is most certain that he is in total control of the direction and the outcome of the affair, and the affair will progress as he sees fit. Some weaker Snakes may find themselves falling in love with a married woman. If this takes place, the power shifts

122

back in her favor, because now she can use his feelings for her to escape the situation or use him off-and-on as she sees fit.

In either case, the ramifications of this kind of extramarital affair usually have a devastating effect on the married woman's family. The reason for this is that the adulterous relationship that she has created outside of her marriage is not "real" at all. It is, in fact, a fantasy driven by the need to feel "alive." No matter how much spin and rationale the married woman puts on the situation, the very root of infidelity is disloyalty. Adultery is based on an "ideal' or fantasy, but it is seldom, if ever, based on reality. Herein lies the danger. On the one hand, she has her very real life, which includes her marriage partner. In this marriage, teamwork, hard work, and ups and downs are simply a part of the marital equation, and through these very real experiences true love is achieved. In this world, children, family, and dreams are the ties that bind the wife to her husband. However, women who cheat on their husbands create a delusional world made up of fantasy and illusion. In this world, deception, secrecy, self-gratification, and betrayal are the ties that bind the wife to the other man. The problem with the woman's infidelity is that no matter if she is engaged in an extramarital affair, or not, she is still bound to her husband. So inevitably, she finds herself caught between two dominant forces, submitting at times to both of them in two different ways in two very different worlds, fantasy, and reality. Consequently, the effects of infidelity have a much more lingering or stain-like affect on the woman than it does the man.

So how much does it cost

When a married woman permits herself to fall into the trappings of an extramarital affair, she sets in motion a chain of chaotic disturbances, that will no doubt, have a destabilizing effect on the family that she has created with her husband. How is a man to know if his woman is even capable of stepping out on him with another man? A clear evaluation of the woman's character should be done at the onset of any relationship. In today's society, women are always checking for "Mr. Right." In many instances, women are not satisfied with their husbands, yet still choose to stay married because they fear being alone. Presented with the right opportunity, many of them would drop their husbands for a newer model, if they could guarantee themselves a better situation. Embracing this kind of wisdom will help many men understand just how easy it is for a Snake with a plan to seduce his woman. Before a woman decides to step out on her husband, she thinks the matter through very carefully. However little, if any, of her final decision is based on pure logic and common practicality. Instead, her decision is usually guided strictly by the need to be emotionally fulfilled. A Snake does not seduce a married woman who does not already want the affair to happen. In other words, these women are in no way shape or form victims. Instead, they are active participants in the possible destruction of their family and marriage. Women often want to believe the flattering words and gestures of a man who is not her husband in order to feel special and appreciated. One must understand that women by nature crave emotional attention from whatever kind of intimate partner they may have in their lives, whether the person is a marriage partner or otherwise. This craving for emotional attention and connection usually stems from an emotional drought that often occurs in many marriages. Emotional droughts occur in most, if not all, marriages at some point in time, simply because as humans, we have a natural tendency to become complacent in our relationships after a significant amount of time has lapsed.

People simply get bored with the same piece of vagina or the same piece of penis, not because either is not good anymore. It is because both are seemingly always present and available during the day-to-day course of a marital relationship. The thrill of the chase and the fear of rejection are seemingly lost elements of the relationship. So, complacency sets in like rigor mortis on a dead body, and ultimately the marriage seems to stiffen with each passing year. During this "stiffening" period, the marriage's emotional intimacy wanes considerably, especially on the part of the husband. It is during this emotionally waning season that most wives start to get restless and start to consider the possibilities of getting more attention from an outside male. Often times when a woman decides to take the plunge into the deep abyss of adultery, she rarely, if ever, takes into account the amount of devastation it will exact on her real life. In other words, most women do not bother to ask, "how, much is this "outside-sex" going to cost?" After an adulterous affair is busted-up by the husband or some other concerned party, the marriage usually goes in one of two directions. Either the marriage is over or salvaged. This is all depending on how far to the left the wife actually went. Maybe she saved a little something respectful enough to

125

salvage, then the reconstruction of the marriage can begin. The reconstruction of a marriage after infidelity is an extremely long and painful process. However, don't be fooled. No matter how much progress the marriage appears to make after infidelity, there are certain "little" intimate things, once exclusively shared within the confines of the marriage that are permanently changed forever.

These things are often the precious pearls used to pay for the affair. Men are naturally territorial beings so actions during the affair that have treaded on their romantic territory are usually the first casualties. A husband who understands a woman's natural need for be emotional support and attention may suspect that she was the first one in the affair to initiate romantic gestures such as holding hands, cuddling, and using affectionate pet names for her fantasy partner. Whether sex has occurred yet or not this is a bad trade on behalf of the wife because husbands see all of her affections as their private romantic territory. These intimate pieces of the marriage are suddenly parceled off in the direction of another man. This is considered a complete act of betrayal. Here is a primary reason why so many husbands upon discovering the wife's extramarital affair, obsess over every small detail of the affair. What the husband really wants to know is; "how much of our private relationship did you give to that snake"? For example, maybe the wife calls her husband "baby" or "sweetheart." In most cases, women who step out on their husbands will use the exact same pet name for her lover in an attempt to connect with them emotionally.

What wives do not comprehend is that when they do this they destroy the "spirit" of the endearing word that once bonded her to her husband. The anger and resentment of the husband is understandable, because most husbands have to "earn" the right to receive their wife's affections through his commitment to his role as "protector" of both her and the family they have created together.

The woman's blind need for emotional attention often times causes her to give away these intimate pieces of her marriage to another man virtually for "free." By doing this, she devalues the terms of endearment that were once used exclusively for her husband. Often times, the goal of the Snake is to influence the married woman to give away as much of her husband's "romantic territory" as possible and this territory is not limited to intimate pet names. Many times these romantic territories can include actual places and things that carry sentimental value and romantic meaning to both husband and wife. Examples of romantic territories in the form of actual places can include places such as, bowling allies, skating rinks, favorite amusement parks, and favorite restaurants. It is like two lions marking their territories by pissing on a nearby tree. The first lion already has laid claim to his territory the second lion comes along and attempts to piss over the first lion's scent mark. Another objective of the Snake is to take away the married woman's options or escape routes. He wants to eliminate the possibility of her getting cold feet and retreating to the safety of her marriage. He accomplishes this by corrupting every good thing in her "real" world so that eventually she will have no one to turn to for comfort and understanding, but him. Therefore, he will make a concerted effort to claim all of the romantic territories of the wife's husband, so that there are indeed no sacred areas that he is unable to access. For instance, he will often suggest and organize a rendezvous with the married woman at these sacred places, in order to begin the process of pushing the husband further and further out of the picture. Once he has sufficiently moved in on all of the romantic places that the wife often shared with her husband, his next move is to screw the woman in her marriage bed. There is no greater conquest of another man's woman, than to get her to sex you down in the same bed that she shares with her husband. This usually takes the skills of a master Snake to pull this stunt off. In most cases, some Snakes have to be satisfied with breaking the woman down outside of her home and merely dreaming of such a complete conquest.

Say My Name

As the extramarital affair gains momentum and the Snake becomes more and more comfortable with the married woman, he will eventually begin to start his, "who is the best" campaign. No matter what type of man is involved in marital infidelity, they all have one thing in common. They all want to know from the woman who is the best. Once again, this is an attempt to get the wife to for lack of a better word, "rat-out" her husband, and uplift the Snake. Now, it really does not matter in the larger scheme of things who is really the best. The husband could in fact be the best lover, however, the purpose for this egotistical campaign is to simply put the married woman between a rock and a hard place by having to dignify the question with a serious answer. If she says the husband is the better of the two in the lovemaking department, she runs the risks of hurting her lover's feelings and possibly ending the fantasy. On the other hand, if she admits that the Snake is indeed a better lover than her husband, she has once again betrayed her husband for the sake of her lover's ego. In either case, no matter what she says she still is caught between a rock and a hard place, which is exactly where the Snake aims to keep her. In the beginning, the Snake is usually just happy to end up having sex with the married chick, but eventually that gratitude will turn into a sense of entitlement as time passes by. As more time elapses he will slowly start to brag openly about how good he is in the sack in spurts, until eventually, he will begin to ask her to co-sign on the fact that he is the best lover she ever had. As his sense of entitlement to her "goodies" grows, the more the married woman loses her freedom to dictate each sexual encounter. During sex with the Snake, the woman will start to notice a shift in the way he treats her sexually. Once attentive and emotionally connected during sex, the Snake now begins to become more and more concerned with being pleased, rather than pleasing. Then finally, after weeks, and months of restraint he blurts out that all too familiar phrase; "what's my name baby?" Now for the first time the married woman realizes that she is in a serious situation. Before while having sex, the Snake was all about pleasing her and talking sweet, asking her if she likes it and is she alright. Now, he's on some "what's my name" tip. So, like a dummy the woman trying not to cause a problem whispers out his name to satisfy his ego, not realizing she just added fuel to the fire. You see the reason why men in general want women to scream out their names during sex is to hear the woman affirm out loud during the experience that, "he is the man" or in fact he is the best and that no other man can compare to him sexually, especially her husband. In the mind of most Snakes, when a woman says his name during sex, it is a clear indication that she is more pleased with his sex than that of her husband despite the fact that she may be saying his name just for kicks. Most Snakes do realize that women may exaggerate sexual pleasure; however, they also understand that regardless of how she truly feels about the sex once she feeds his ego by saying his name she can never take it back once again she has chosen him over her husband. You see, unlike the husband who perceives the wife as an extension of himself and is bound to the woman in marriage for better or for worse, the Snake has no such perception he is only bound to her in secrecy and sees her as a source of free sex with no strings attached.

In his mind he is thinking, "Why should I bother going out to the club and risk rejection from women when I can get some free sex from this married man's wife?" Therefore, ever so slowly the Snake begins to breakdown every sacred sexual and romantic barrier that may have existed between him and the married woman. Once each one of these barriers have been eliminated, he gains full access to parts of her that were once only reserved for her husband. In many cases, the wife simply hands these intimate parts of herself over to the Snake without any form of guilt or second thought.

My Stuff!

When the relationship reaches this level the Snake once again asserts himself, and now seeks more than her approval of his sexual prowess. Now he wants to take ownership of her body, so he becomes increasingly aggressive and self-confident during sex with the woman, until sure enough he pops the big question on her, "whose stuff is this?" This is a direct challenge to her loyalty to her husband and an indirect challenge to her husband, in general, insofar as who she sexually belongs to. "Whose stuff is this?" is just another way the Snake is trying to say, "I don't want you "sexing" anybody else, but me and that includes your husband". However ironic, by posing this unrealistic question, he is actually petitioning the married woman to remain exclusive to him sexually. It always comes down to this, or something like this in some shape or form where the woman is eventually called out and pressured to choose who she is really "down" with. A woman's power in any relationship lies in her right to "choose" a man that she is going to be down with. She may be able to postpone the process of choosing, for as long as it is possible. Inevitably, she will always be compelled to choose between two men, because nature will not allow her to have both.

Rule #5
His Trash is Your Treasure

It can be an awkward moment in a friendship between two men when one of them falls for the other's ex-girlfriend. The first reason being is that most men are instinctively territorial over women. It is just that simple. No matter how long a man has been away from a woman that he has an established sexual history with, he still feels a deep sense of "ownership" over her sexuality. If you add a love element to that kind of relationship, then it really does not matter if a man is still with the woman or not. He still somehow feels that she will always belong to him.

The best way to deal with such a dilemma is for the two friends to make an agreement. This agreement should include a pact that discourages fallouts over women, period. Men who cry over an ex-girlfriend, wife, etc. are weak, because regardless, she will eventually become intimate with another man, period, whether he is a friend of her ex or not. A man who gets upset with a friend for getting with his ex is being unrealistic and unfair because often times the woman is just as interested in her ex-man's friend, as the fried is in her. Therefore, many times the woman is the initiator of the situation in the first place. Some men in this circumstance are often hypocritical, because they will often tolerate the ex woman with any man, other than his best friend. She could be with a dude that beats her, takes advantage of her etc. As long as she does not choose to be with his friend, anyone else is acceptable. To be fair, many women choose to be with the friend of their ex because they have become familiar with the friend's character. She views him as more of a safe bet or alternative to starting over from scratch. Outside of any form of selfishness on her part, this is actually a calculated decision based on facts that she knows about the ex's best friend.

133

Secondly, if one of the friends becomes remotely interested in his homeboy's ex girl, then the woman should be honest about it and have an open about it and have an open discussion about the possibilities of getting with the friend. By doing this, she is accepting responsibility for her new choice. In theory if this conversation makes the ex feel uncomfortable or strikes up feelings of anger or resentment, the best thing to do is kill the whole situation, simply because a piece of booty is not worth two friends falling out over. However, a woman's instinct often guides her decision in these instances and often trumps any form of being socially or politically correct. If she feels that the friend makes her feel more secure, loved, respected etc. then she will usually make a decision based on her natural feelings for the friend. In such a circumstance, the men should to come to an agreement and concur that the ex-girl is fair game. Nevertheless, this could signal the beginning of the end of a life-long friendship. The chief rule of thumb in this type of situation is to try not to fall in love with your homeboy's ex-girl, period, because it can be awkward. If it is a physical attraction, let it stop at that. You see, the woman is not going to feel the awkwardness, as strongly as you will. In her eyes, the main attraction may be the fact that she has managed to have two friends. Be careful because some women are more attracted to the situation, than the individual. Meaning, the act of being intimate with two men who know each other turns her on more than the men in the situation. It is the same sense of power and dominance that men feel when they have sex with two sisters either at the same time or at different intervals. Men wear that type of conquest like a badge of

134

honor. Well, some women do the same thing, when it comes to getting with two men who are friends. Never forget that women are just as, if not more, clever than men when it comes to these relationship issues. Underestimating a woman's motives will often times lead to catastrophic consequences in the lives of men.

Here are a couple of things to remember about women and their motives. Fact, women enjoy sex just as much as men. However, what you must realize is that women are far more imaginative and often times more innovative than men in the game of love and sex. From the time most women spot two male friends who are single, she already knows which of them she wants to screw and which of them she would prefer to have stick around merely for companionship and material purposes.

My roommate's girl

Case and point, while attending college I became roommates with a friend of mine. He and I had become cool with each other. I thought a lot about the guy because he was a really good-hearted individual. He had his own apartment in the city. I was in between living conditions, so he asked me to move in with him until I got on my feet. So, I did. He had just started dating this girl on campus and she was cool with the move. In the beginning everything was "aight," no problems at all, we would go to class, come home and chill. He and his girl would stay locked up in their room most of the time. I would have my female friends over, as well. One day I was at the crib by myself studying and heard a knock at the door it was my roommate's girl, so I let her in. Something immediately dawned on me about her visit. It was just a little too unusual. She knew her man's schedule like clockwork therefore, she knew that he was still in class and would not be home for hours. Another thing was how she was dressed, she had an average cute face and this woman's body was "banging." She had gotten herself all fixed up in some tight little pastel shorts that clung to her hips like latex paint looking good. She also wore a halter-top that exposed her tightly crafted mid-drift. It was a warm day outside, so she had a very light sheen of sweat all over her well-shaped legs and arms mixed with glitter body lotion that sparkled in contrast against her coffee brown skin. As a former High School athlete, I had not seen a body on a woman so well defined and beautiful as hers since track season. It didn't take long to figure out what was up. I played it off though and just talked to her, she was a good talker. Now I consider myself a sharp brotha when it comes to matching wits with people, but this woman was just as clever and sharp as I was, if not more. In my head I was like wow, this girl is mackin me like I'm a chick! It got hard for me not to accept her challenge because I started feeling like if I did not step up and handle my business I might be perceived as some kind of "wuss" or something. She kept placing herself in my path everywhere I went in that tiny apartment until finally I moved towards the kitchen and there she met me at the entrance and stood there knowing I had to walk by her. When I finally walked by she carefully pushed her tightly rounded "bootylicious" into my crotch, I instantaneously got hard as a rock. It took everything in me from grabbing her by the wrist and walking her through the hall into my bedroom and giving her what I knew she wanted.

Instead, like a straight up "punk." I cleared my throat and asked her what was up with her and my roommate. *Was everything cool*? I questioned. She answered and said with a serious look; *"I am not really attracted to him I am attracted to you"*. She went on to say how he was not her type and so-on. Now, this girl and I did have a little history of friendship before she started dating my "boy," which made it even harder to resist her obvious charm. We would often be on the verge of "hooking-up" but it seemed like circumstances played more of a role with us not making a connection than anything else.

Needless to say I found a way to not end up screwing my roommate's girl, even though she was down for creeping. I can't lie; I was down too just not at the cost of backstabbing a friend who extended a helping hand to me when I was in need of a place to live. I was many things back then, but being ungrateful was not one of them. As I said circumstances! I simply knew that the right thing to do was to respect my homeboy and not snake him behind his back. Afterwards, I could sense that she did not want me around much, after I avoided her advances. She began to cause problems between us (at least I suspect she did) until I finally moved on out. I did not hate her for trying me, because aside from being flattered and wanting to get at her myself, I knew why she was with him in the first place. She was with him because he had "financial means"; therefore, he could take care of her the way she wanted to be taken care of. I, on the other hand, was simply a "broke" college student. It is just that simple. Now some may ask why I did not tell him what went down, if he was such a good friend

That type of situation is far more complex than one would imagine. The first thing is that this guy was in LOVE, and I mean, in love with this woman. She had this brotha so whipped. I swear he would have gone crazy, if I told him such a thing. When a man is "whipped" and he is in love there ain't a thing in the world short of him seeing with his own eyes that will convince him otherwise. I simply moved on quietly and wished him well. This is what I mean when I say that a woman always knows who she wants to have sex with as opposed to whom she wants to pay her bills. As soon as I moved in, this woman knew that if I was down she could have the best of both worlds, so to speak.

In the end, however, you have to be a man about it. Respect the game and do not violate what your friend believes to be true about his situation, regardless of what you may think the status of his relationship is with his girl. You see, your friend believes that his world, which includes his woman, is a "certain way"; that is his reality. You violate his reality when you inform him that you are now flying in violation of his airspace.

If you do happen to find yourself in a sexual relationship with your best friend's ex-girl then you must follow the rules that apply to such an intrinsically awkward relationship. There are schools of thought out there that say, "if your friend cannot hang on to his lady then you must be manlier in her eyes in order for her to choose you." Another theory is; "if your boy isn't with her anymore then she is fair game." Let me address both schools of thought one be one. First, a woman has various reasons for dumping one man and choosing another. These days you have to be careful because plenty of women are dumping men who they deem to be overly masculine and domineering and choose to be in a relationship

138

where they feel more in control, insofar as their ability to pilot the relationship in a direction more suitable for themselves.

In other words, the woman might have chosen you over the man she dumped, not because you are more of a man but maybe because you are in her eyes less of one, easily controllable and gullible to her wishes and wants. The fair game theory is another school of thought often espoused by some. It states that once your boy and his girl split, then she is now fair game. That kind of logic is only true in part. Yes she is fair game, but only if she is willing to inform her ex about the situation. When your best friend decides to get involved intimately with your ex, several other factors become a part of that kind of situation. First off, your "boy" now becomes privy to your entire sexual history with your ex-girlfriend which may include her true opinions of your character that she may not have dared to share with you out of concern for your feelings. Now with you out of the picture, she now begins to confide in your best friend about your personal issues.

Rule #6

All wives have a past

Many men are one hundred percent sold on the idea that their woman is virtuous. This is due, in part, to the fact that from the onset of most relationships, women go out of their way to either cover up their sexual past or downplay it as much as possible. A woman who talks a great deal, about what she has never done sexually with other men is attempting to control how her new man views her, because she is aware that his perception of her will dictate how much he values her. A man must always come to terms with the fact that his woman has a past and there are always a couple of men in her past that have either sexed her to the point of shame and embarrassment, or to the point of ecstasy. In either case, most women will not disclose the true details of either. A man who thinks that his penis is enough to keep his woman from wanting to have sex with another man is an arrogant fool. The fact is that the majority of women are given over to their passions and vices, much the same as men are. Most men do not bother investigating a woman's past because they are all too obsessed with the desire of wanting to have sex with her at all costs. This is a risky way to go about establishing a long-term relationship with a woman. There are fundamental details that must be addressed before you dive head first into any meaningful relationship with her.

The very first thing you should do is a "background" check. However, do not ask her female friends because women can be unreliable character witnesses for each other. You never can know what other women truly feel about your girl because their motives cannot be trusted. The best thing to do is ask other men that know her.

Find out what their opinion is of her character. Be sure to ask men from her neighborhood or hometown. These guys may know a side of her that you haven't seen yet. The responses that you get from these men will be useful in your final analysis of her. If a guy tells you "she's alright" that usually means he doesn't know much about her, and that she maintains a low profile, or it could just mean that he is "hating" on you and doesn't want to see you get with her period. Do not take this as an automatic "good sign" because this could mean different things such as she prefers a low profile because she is "sneaky" and does her dirt on the low. If you keep running into people who do not know much about your girl, this is a clue that you need to take it slow until you are able to find out more about her character. If a man says she is "stuck up." this could be a good sign because most men use this term for women who simply reject or ignore them. If she has never acted "stuck up" to you by rejecting you then this obviously means that you are the "chosen one" in her eyes. You see, a woman's natural instinct is to reject unwanted male attention and unwanted males in general; therefore, this could work in your favor.

A woman who has the reputation of being one of the guys is either a "Hoe or gay." If your girl has, a whole bunch of male friends that she used to just "kick it with." then be mindful that she may enjoy the company of various males a little too much. If none of those male friends have ever had sex with her you could be dealing with a bisexual or straight up gay female who is trying to work out her sexual identity while she is with you. Generally speaking, all straight men when given the opportunity will eventually get around to having sex with a woman even if they are the best of friends. That is just the way straight men are made. If a couple of her male friends have had sex with her, then she has gotten used to the idea of having more than one male sex partner. In any case, this does not bode well for your attempt to make her exclusively yours in marriage. The more sexual partners a woman has before settling down and getting married makes her more likely to commit infidelity against her husband simply because she has developed an appetite for sexual variety. A woman, who feeds on this assorted diet, usually has no problem justifying her behavior through society's acceptance of it. This can bring her to the point where, on a subconscious level, having sex exclusively with her husband becomes illogical. After you have asked people about her, you should at least, have a good idea of what her public reputation was in her past amongst her peers.

Now you must dig a little deeper. Get to know everything you can about the women in her family, especially her mother. Many men do not pay enough attention to genetics, but it can mean the difference between a marriage full of love and understanding and a marriage full of confusion. Point blank, if your wife's mother was a "Freak" in her day, you are in a lot of trouble. This kind of information is going to be hard to come by, initially because your woman is going to want you to see her mother in a positive light and she may not be aware of her mother sexual past either. The best starting point is to inquire about the other women in her family more specifically her aunts. (If her mother has any sisters) Most mothers will not tell their daughters all the dirt they have done in their past, but they are more likely to air out Aunt Betty's dirty laundry. Your woman should know if she has a couple freaky aunts in her family. When pulling this kind of information out of her you must be tasteful and nonjudgmental or she will surely clam up on you. The key to getting this kind of precious background information on the sexual past of your future wife's people is to get your girl to do the sleuthing for you. Get her to ask her mom about the other women in her family. This will open up the mother to discuss her personal sexual past with the daughter as well. If your girl comes from a long line of women in her family that cheat on their husbands, or were sexually promiscuous as single women, then the chances that your woman is the same way is very high. The more you are able to learn and know about the mother the more accurately you will be able to determine exactly what type of woman you are dealing with.

Rule #7
Always a Double Standard

Why do men get so enraged and upset when they find out their wives or girlfriends have stepped out on them? Why is the reaction to infidelity so fundamentally different between men and women? Women have always complained that there is an obvious double standard when it comes to female infidelity. Many women emphatically suggest that men are too unreasonable when the wife's indiscretion is exposed, while women on the other hand are far more forgiving and less inclined to end the marriage or relationship when their male counterparts get busted for stepping out. The reason why there is such a sharp difference in the way men and women respond to infidelity cannot be adequately addressed strictly based on socialization. The man's extremely hostile attitude towards his woman's infidelity is more of a biological reaction or basic instinct than anything else. There are certain instinctive human responses that are designed to protect us from harm perceived or otherwise. These instinctive responses are not so easily subdued simply by being a part of a so-called "civilized society." The blind fury, rage, and obsessive behavior of a man who has discovered his wife' infidelity is no different from the blind fury, rage, and anger of a woman who discovers that her children have been harmed by a stranger. In other words, the only thing equivalent to the anger of a woman who is defending her children from danger is the anger and fury of a husband who believes his wife is seeing another man. In both of these cases, the men and women react with the same kind of irrational behavior and obsessive need for vengeance. You can take the kindest, most sophisticated, docile woman and turn her into a raging lioness if you mess with her kids.

146

A woman instinctively cannot fathom the thought of witnessing her child suffer hurt, harm or danger at the hands of a stranger. If pushed to this point, her natural instincts will most certainly take over and she will kill if necessary to protect her child.

Likewise, most men cannot fathom the thought of his wife sexing another man. He will instinctively feel the need to protect both his manhood and bloodline from the threat and interference of an outside male. This is the major difference between how men and women view female initiated infidelity. A wife who engages in an extramarital affair, no matter what precautions she takes always runs the risk of getting pregnant by the other man. Many DNA laboratories are starting to see a sharp increase in the number of paternity tests coming back showing that 30 percent of men tested are not really the biological fathers of their children and are unaware of this fact. Statistics also reveal that nearly forty percent of married women cheat on their husbands frequently and that percentage is steadily rising. This risk is not just a threat to her marriage, but it is a direct threat to the continuation of her husband's "true" bloodline. This is the root of her husband's reaction to her infidelity. A married woman who bares the child of another man often times does not share this information with her husband.

In today's society, more and more men unknowingly are raising children that do not biologically belong to them. These children serve absolutely, no biological purpose to the husband because they can in no way carry on his genetic bloodline. Instead, they will bring forth the descendants of the very individual that his wife betrayed him. A man's hostile reaction and low tolerance for female infidelity is an instinct provided to him by nature. This instinct is designed to protect his ability to procreate and bring forth children of his own lineage, which in turn improves the chances of survival for his specific genetic bloodline. If there is indeed, a double standard existing between men and women when it comes to the issue of infidelity, the standard was created by nature not society. You see many women misinterpret their husband's reaction to their infidelity. Many times in order to explain why men are more hostile and intolerant of female-initiated infidelity women come up with absurd theories such as men see them as property like a car or favorite watch.

Contrary to popular belief, men do not see women as property. Men see their wives as a direct extension of themselves; therefore, when a husband feels another man has compromised the chastity of his wife. He takes that indiscretion as a direct assault on his manhood rather than a simple mistake or act of emotional weakness on behalf of his wife. This is why many husbands become obsessed about every single detail of the affair once it has been exposed. Women may think that the husband is simply jealous and upset but the main issue the husband is most concerned with is how much of herself the wife actually offered to the other man.

The husband is mostly concerned about how much of his inadequacies were shared with the stranger and how much of his personal life (manhood) he can retrieve after the fact. You see the husband feels more vulnerable, than jealous. Secondly, the husband always wants to know one thing, and that is "did you go down him"? If a wife has given oral sex to another man she may as well file for divorce, because whether or not the marriage survives the initial blow of the affair, the marriage will forever be haunted by this one dreaded detail, especially if the married couples are black. Black men see the act of oral sex as a form of absolute submission on the part of the black woman, therefore if a black wife gives oral sex to her secret lover, in the eyes of her husband she has given up every part of herself to the other man leaving nothing left to salvage in the relationship.

For many years black women have been known to be sexually conservative, strong-willed and initially unwilling to give her man "head" in the initial stages of a relationship. Black men would have to earn his woman's respect first before she would bless his manhood with this kind of absolute submission. Even in today's society where some black women are starting to explore and imitate the progressively decadent culture of America, there are still a vast majority of black women who maintain a standard of sexual conservatism that has long since defined and separated them from other women in American society.

In other words, a black man internalizes and interprets the adulterous behavior of his woman a little differently. He does not view her outside of himself, instead he considers her to be a part of his "very being" not as a trivial piece of property. Consequently, he views her infidelity as a total act of betrayal against his manhood and in turn perceives the other man as a "violator" of an unspoken truce that exists among men. Upon realizing this, it becomes quite evident why a woman's infidelity places the marriage and family on shaky ground. No matter what the social or politically climate of the day is, humans are still governed by the laws of nature, and these laws usually dictate the social dynamics that exist between men and women. Therefore, there will always be a difference in the way men and women view female-initiated infidelity.

No matter how independent a woman is in society, when she agrees to have sex with a man other than her husband, she is in a direct conflict with her husband's role as the dominant male in her life. No woman can submit herself to the will of two men at the same time, without being pulled in two opposite directions. She will ultimately choose one and neglect the other. Furthermore, two men cannot occupy the same space in a women's life this will ultimately lead to confusion and internal conflict on behalf of the woman. In other words, two dominant forces cannot exist within the same space for long without eventually changing the space altogether. The space I am referring to is the heart of the woman. You see, in order for most women to fall head first into a full-blown extramarital affair she has to emotionally, begin to connect with the other man on some level. She has to bring herself to the point where she puts more and more of her heart into the affair.

A woman that goes about the business of having an extramarital affair by default has invited a stranger into the lives of her entire family, which may include her children. The major problem with this is that it breads confusion and undermines the role of her husband in her family. In contrast, most wives do realize that if given the opportunity, most men will screw another woman but are less likely to get attached emotionally. Women generally understand that men pursue them purely for physical sex and are more reluctant to get involved with a mistress on an emotional level. This understanding serves as a kind of barometer for wives allowing them to measure just how serious of a threat the other woman is and to what extent the affair went. When a husband steps out on his wife emotions will run high, but the wife usually wants to know two things; one is "Do you love her?" The second thing is, "How does she look?" Once the husband affirms that, he was just banging the chick, the marriage usually is out of danger. This is not to imply that he may not get slapped. I'm just saying that, in most cases, once a women realizes that the other woman is no real threat to her place in her husband's heart the wife will find a place to put the situation. However, if he does reveal that he has fallen in love with the other woman the wife's response can be just as hostile and irrational as a man's, in most cases, because now she feels that her family is threatened by an outsider.

The husband on the other hand has no such barometer, he knows beyond a shadow of a doubt that if his wife has had sex with another man outside of their marriage, she has put not only a great deal of thought into the matter, but she has also opened herself up emotionally to another man. She has given this other man access to piece of her heart that was once reserved only for him. Men know that women are emotional creatures, and in order to get a woman to throw away her morality, one must connect with them on an emotional level first. The main thing that distinguishes male and female infidelity is that most husbands who sleep around with a woman on the side usually keep the mistress at a safe distance from his "real" family and life.

151

Black men who choose to have a woman on the side will often times choose one who is younger than his wife, preferably a single mother and of a lower economic status than himself. By choosing a woman of this type, the man is creating a relationship with a woman that is based primarily on "dependency." The young mistress may well have fallen in love with the married man, but he still makes sure to give her a little something for the bills every month just to keep her satisfied.

The fact that she is a young single mother protects the wife's role as the dominant female. Therefore, the mistress has little, if no leverage in the relationship which in theory makes her less inclined to challenge for the wife's position. Consequently, the husband does not have to worry about the stress of having to "promise" to leave his wife just to keep the affair going. However, due to the mistress's dependency and subordinate social status the secrecy of the "affair" becomes just as necessary for the mistress as it is to the husband. A man who is an "alpha male" does not tolerate his mistress "over-stepping" her boundaries. These types of men will create rules of engagement when it comes down to an extramarital affair such as: The mistress is never allowed to call his home for any reason at anytime. She is not permitted to visit his home at all. The mistress is not allowed to talk extensively about the wife or to the wife directly. A mistress that takes it upon herself to keep discussing the wife will usually get verbally assaulted and chastised by the man. A mistress is often required to be exclusive to her married man and is forbidden to engage in sexual intercourse with other men. Finally, a mistress is usually required to cater to the needs of the husband with as much attentiveness, if not more than the wife. She is expected to cook for him, wash his clothes, give him money, screw him, and console him, if needed. So in essence when a dominant man takes a mistress to be his other woman she actually morphs into the role of "second-wife ."

Harmony vs. Equality

Another difference is based simply on the very different roles men and women play in a relationship. Infidelity ultimately affects how well both the husband and the wife play these defined roles that have been ascribed to us by nature. A relationship should be based on "harmony" not equality. We achieve this harmony when we accept our roles without trying to change them. We must understand that a man's role should be that of the "dominant" force in the relationship and the women's role should be that of the "passive" force. The largely white lesbian feminist agenda in American society has pushed all women to the brink of an all out war of the sexes. Women in our society no longer see men as partners instead; they are slowly beginning to see men as the enemy or adversaries. As each decade passes, the relationship between men and women becomes increasingly more adversarial.

Feminists declare that men and women should be "equal" in a marriage relationship. As far back as the ice age, white men have always dominated their women by force and brute strength. During the time of the

Neanderthal cave man era in Europe, the woman was not a valued member of the clan. She was not loved and adored. She was simply a tool used for breeding. When the caveman wanted to mate with a woman, he simply knocked her over the head and dragged her off to the cave to handle his business. Even during the glory days of nations such as Greece and Rome, the woman still could not catch a break. The majority of Roman, Greek, Spartan, Macedonian aristocrats and soldiers gave much more respect and attention to their young male lovers, whom they often used as sex slaves, than to the wives they had at home. Still, in these "civilized" societies the white woman's worth was only tied to her ability to breed. Down through the ages the white woman has always had to be a second-class citizen in her white man's world. Even in early American history, white women where not allowed to own property, vote, or work in some states. The white man ruled his woman with his boot on her neck, keeping her empty and insignificant while gorging himself with the blood of conquered peoples and enjoying the spoils of his destruction. White feminism was born out of a hatred for white manhood this is why white women are so obsessed with the idea of being "equal"! The word "equal" often implies "sameness" or to suggest that two people or things are the same or should be the same. On the contrary, no two things in the universe are the same. You can take two identical twins that to the naked eye appear to look the same, and yet break them down genetically and discover that they are very much different. Thus, their identical appearance is an "illusion." not a reality. In the United States of America, our justice system implies that there is equal justice for all, when in fact American justice is nothing more than a concept of fairness. In reality, there is no such thing as equal justice because the word equality alone gives the false impression that all people are the same, when in fact all people are very different.

You cannot take the politically-correct idea and illusion of equality and apply it to a marriage, because a union between a man and a woman is not based on some ambiguous concept of equality. The union is based on balance or harmony, the bringing together of two distinctly different people and creating a whole. This whole or harmony occurs when both individuals play their designated roles in the relationship. Within a musical harmony, often times there are many different notes played by the musician simultaneously. Each one of these notes has a designated sound or responsibility. No two notes share the "same" sound. It is the job of the musician to figure out and execute the process of bringing all of these different notes together in order to create one whole sound. A good marriage operates much the same way. Each person brings his or her unique differences to the relationship and creates harmony.

Signs

First off, let me say this, there are always signs that your woman is either thinking about sleeping around on you or "is" sleeping" around on you. Most men however, are so caught up in the day-to-day things going down in the world that we miss most if not all of these signs. Therefore, here is a rule, never ever trust your woman

155

One hundred percent, no matter how long you have been with her. No matter if, a woman considers herself happily married or not, she loves it when a single dude tries to holla at her. Any man who thinks that his woman is too precious or too special to sleep around on him is seriously misguided. The common rule of thumb is that the more convinced you are of your women's virtue, the less virtue she actually has. You should always understand why your woman would want to betray you with another man. This calls for deep self-analysis on your part. You must set aside your ego and admit to yourself your shortcomings. This is because your woman, nine times out of ten, is already aware of your shortcomings, no matter how hard you may have tried not to expose them. In other words, you must calculate the risk factor of your wife committing infidelity, along with just how much of a role your shortcomings may play in it. There is no one reason why married women commit adultery. There are usually several reasons that may produce this kind of behavior. Women are complex people; therefore, one must take into account the various circumstances that may lead a married woman down this path.

Some women cheat on their husbands because it is, in fact, a family behavioral pattern passed down from mother to daughter down through each generation. In these types of situations, the woman is usually racked with guilt and confusion during adulterous affairs, while simultaneously she feels a need or an impulse to continue flirting with other men behind her husband's back. The confusion comes from the fact that she is not clearly certain why she is doing it. She just feels as if something is compelling her to do it. After getting busted by their husbands, many of these women usually say that they do not know exactly what they were thinking of or they didn't know why they decided to go through with the act of sexual intimacy with another man. As ironic as it sounds, they are actually as confused and mystified as their husbands when the question of "why" is raised. A woman who has a long family history of adulterous behavior usually will feel that while the "affair" is in progress, it has a hint of familiarity to it or it feels normal, as if she is supposed to do it. Only afterwards, does the confusion and guilt settle in.

This woman really wants to be faithful, however she feels magnetically attracted to this type of situation. If you are married to a woman such as this, the best course of action is to get your wife to confront her past and deal with it before any "real" reconciliation can take place. If your woman simply promises never to "screw" around again and you neglect to investigate her family's past, she will ultimately keep repeating the same behavior.

I need some Attention

Oftentimes, a woman will feel neglected or under appreciated by her husband. This is a prime reason why most women step outside of their marriage and engage in an adulterous affair. A woman who believes that her husband is no longer paying attention to her emotionally will begin to consider the possibility of finding another man to pay her some attention. Women, by nature, are emotional beings, therefore, when they feel that their emotional needs aren't being met they almost always start to seek out those who would feed their need for emotional comfort and support. Women usually seek the emotional support of other close female friends. They will start to spend an inordinate amount of time talking to these friends on the phone. This is a sign that she is detaching herself from her husband and starting to "cling" more closely to her friends for emotional support. However, here is the "clincher." If your woman starts to suddenly, make new female friends on the job, then you had better take notice. When a woman starts to dig up a new best friend every other week or month this is a clear sign that she is reaching out to others for emotional support and becoming more indiscriminate as time passes.

Eventually, she will not limit herself to making friends with strictly people of the female persuasion. Gradually she will become more open to the idea that other men could be a better source of platonic emotional support and comfort. Once she has embraced this kind of thinking she will systematically start to eliminate her new female best friends. By doing this, she is making room for the possibility of embarking on an emotional affair with another man. Some women simply get flat out bored with married life and actively seek out other men to add a little adventure to their lives. It is no secret that most marriages will eventually level off and reach a peak during the lifetime of the relationship. To the bored wife, this is a sentence worse than death. She cannot fathom the thought of being trapped in a "leveled off" relationship where monotony has become commonplace. She craves excitement and is in love with the idea of being in love more than being in a marriage. Women, such as

These, get restless and seek to recapture a time when they felt good about themselves.

These kind of women cannot be stopped. They are going to sleep around no matter what. It is just a matter of time. One of the first signs that your woman is thinking about cheating on you is a subtle change in her appearance or dress. Now these changes are ever so subtle, so pay careful attention. Many women who work in a professional environment will change their hairstyle to reflect a more girlish youthful appearance in order to attract the attention of the other man. One of the main hair- styles of choice is the ever-popular "pony-tail." For sistas who do not have extremely long hair, this is no obstacle they simply will purchase a hair weave piece from the local beauty supply to achieve this look of choice. Another popular hairstyle is the "Shirley temple" curls.

These are two of the main hairstyles cheating woman flaunt to get attention. Your woman may also put blond streaks in her hair also. These hairstyles are usually not considered professional. If your woman is going to work with this new "do" you better wake up and pay attention. The second sign may be an over interest in her cleavage. She will begin to either purchase clothing or drag out blouses that accentuate her breast and wear them to work. At times, you may catch her daydreaming more frequently than usual. If you have an older daughter and your wife starts to borrow her clothes to wear out, then you'd better start paying attention. If you are a younger couple and your wife starts to borrow clothes from her younger sister or niece, pay attention.

159

Things such as open toed sandals, anklets, and bright red nail polish on the hands and feet are all signs as well. A few subtle, but very reliable sign that your woman is involved with a little side action going on may be constipation. Many times stress can cause constipation, and this may cause bad breath. She may try to mask this by suddenly purchasing gum and mints on a regular basis. Women who cheat on their husbands usually become stressed out during the process of concealing the whole affair, thus as a result she becomes constipated more frequently. Premature aging is usually a symptom that occurs among women who have spent nearly a lifetime cheating on their husbands. The intense long-term emotional strain of having to keep the affair a secret is extremely stressful and has a tendency to cause women to get sick more often as well, as to appear to grow older prematurely as time passes.

Lastly, she may start to hide the cell phone bills and become increasingly secretive about her phone calls. The home phone may start to ring at odd times, and the person on the other end may hang up on you when you answer. She may often leave the room or go outside to answer her cell, at times. She will make up excuses that will enable her to leave the house and run small errands that she usually would not want to make. On occasion, some women will unwittingly admit that there is a man at work who may be showing an interest in her. She will not go out of her way to convince you of this, but she may only mention it in passing so you better listen. The reason women do this it to start creating an alibi. If her unfaithfulness is discovered the cheating wife always wants to be able to say that she did not mean for it to happen and that it all took her by surprise. When the husband does not believe her, she will gladly remind him of the time she mentioned the Snake and that if she had intended for the affair to happen she would have never mentioned him in his presence. Therefore, she implies that if the husband had a problem with it, he should have said so when she mentioned the guy's name in the first place. Check this. When a married woman steps outside of her marriage she willingly does so, for whatever reason. Her instincts tell her that she is dead wrong and that she is committing a sort of marital suicide like anyone who is contemplating suicide, there are always signs and cries for help before anything actually happens. This is why most women usually casually mention the name of the Snake in the presence of her husband before any real infidelity takes place. It is up to the husband to recognize when his wife is about to commit marital suicide.

Rule #8
Change the Rules Change the Structure

Polygamy: Black America's Solution

For centuries, America has systematically controlled the moral consciousness of black Americans through public policies and propaganda designed to influence what black folks consider appropriate or acceptable. For example, in the past predominately white churches formed mega churches and preached the doctrine of prosperity long before the TD Jakes' and Creflo Dollars of today. Only when it became obvious that black preachers were starting to make as much money as the white super Evangelist, did the government step in and begin to aggressively change and challenge the 'tax-exempt" status of all churches. It is no secret that for decades, blacks were sold the idea that filing for bankruptcy was the worst thing on the earth for anyone. However, whites were filing for bankruptcy left and right on a regular basis and seemingly at will securing additional loans in no time at all. However, it became a National problem, once blacks caught on and began to utilize the same financial alternative. In response, the government changed the bankruptcy laws in order to make it more difficult to file for bankruptcy.

The point here is that American Society has no moral ground to stand on and is in no moral position to judge or dictate to African-Americans seeking to improve and repair their community through the honorable institution of polygamous marriage. Blacks who even allow this corrupt society we live in today to sway their minds against this natural form of family that has been apart of human history since the dawn of man are foolish. White America outlaws or criticizes anything until they can fully understand how to benefit from it. Once they figure out a way to benefit from it, all of a sudden it becomes legal or at least morally acceptable.

Early during American history, alcohol used to be as illegal to possess, as "crack cocaine." The government used tough prohibition laws, churches, newspapers, and the educational system as vehicles into the homes and minds of its citizens in order to create a "guilt-consciousness" towards the consumption and possession of simple alcohol. This guilt-consciousness was driven by the fear of legal and social persecution. It was not until some smart guy in the government figured out that they could make a whole bunch of money by creating an alcohol tax, that the government reversed its hostile position against the sale and consumption of alcohol. Consequently, the entire moral consciousness of the average American changed seemingly as fast as the law changed itself.

You better believe that if white women in America faced a man shortage as black women do today, the laws on the books concerning polygamy would be rewritten. Overnight, the practice would become not only legal, but nationally celebrated as a divine gift of mercy to the white family in America. National religious figures would all of a sudden hail polygamy as a victory for white womanhood and key religious personalities would be used to make the whole idea morally acceptable to white Americans. All the while black folk would be left sitting on the outside looking in, while white families gleefully rebuild themselves using the intrinsically African practice of polygamy. Much of the social stigma surrounding the idea of polygamy is unfair and driven by the American social system which promotes European ideas such as feminism, homosexuality, and monogamy. Traditionally, the American social system has slandered intrinsically African family structures such as polygamy in order to preserve a Western European style society. The European theology of Christianity takes the position that the natural relationship between a man and a woman is inherently sinful and only necessary for procreation. Christianity often glorifies male celibacy or abstinence from sex with a female and views marriage as some sort of last, ditch effort to avoid the temptation of sex between men and women. According to the Bible, Paul writes in 1st Corinthians, chapter 7, verses 1 and 2;

(1) "It is good for a man not to touch a woman. (2) Never the less, to avoid fornication, let every man have his own wife, and let every woman have her own husband."

This kind of religious reasoning leaves the door open to deviant sexual practices, because it admonishes people to view the sex between a man and a woman as sinful, while leaving no clear alternatives other than marriage by default, abstinence, or homosexuality. This is part of the reason we have deviant sexual behavior and feminism running rampant in churches. Individuals under the spell of these negative behaviors are slowly molding and shaping a new theological and social agenda for the Christian church as a whole in order to justify their delinquent state of mind.

You see, both European Jews and Christians have one thing in common. Both share the belief that the intrinsically Afro-Hebraic practice of polygamy is morally corrupt. While other lifestyles such as male homosexuality and lesbianism should be tolerated, explored, endorsed,

165

debated, and even incorporated into mainstream American life. Proposals such as "same sex marriage" are now being debated and entertained in the courtrooms and legislative halls of America and even some churches.

Finally, who pays the price for this kind of social hypocrisy and moral decay? Our black families pick up the tab, of course, especially our women. Black women pay the price for buying the American dream. Their children remain fatherless, and they remain without husbands. Many of our women are now turning to each other for intimacy by the thousands, as result. The number of our women choosing to take their clothes off in strip clubs just to pay the bills is rising, yet they buy the American Pie called monogamy. Can we blame them? Where are the men? Many of our women will never become wives because "sorry men" made them content with being every other man's "baby's momma" which is nothing more than "Defacto-polygamy" at best.

Ghetto Polygamy

The difference between *defacto-polygamy* and *ghetto polygamy* is that ghetto polygamy is more like man sharing than anything else. However, it places the woman at a disadvantage because it does not offer her the security that traditional polygamy offers. Polygamy offers her the security of knowing that her man values her as a wife instead of just a "baby-momma." Still man-sharing or ghetto polygamy is usually an honest attempt by a black man to consolidate his baby momma drama and a desperate attempt by black women for companionship. Despite these attempts, ghetto polygamy often does not foster loyalty by the man to the woman and vice versa.

Hence, women in this position often feel justified to sleep around with other men, while in their ghetto polygamous relationships. This often leads to an escalation of sexually transmitted diseases in the black community.

Defacto-polygamy occurs when black boys make babies with multiple black women and are unable to or refuse to take care of either the child or the woman instead leaving the responsibility of rearing the family to the government. A man practicing ghetto polygamy at least realizes that it is much cheaper and a lot more manageable, if he can get all of the mothers of his children to work together with him by finding a suitable place for all them to live and work out their differences under one roof. Ghetto polygamy (with an emphasis on loyalty) is probably the most practical form of polygamy that could actually be implemented in the black community today, because it addresses an immediate demand for the children involved to be under the protection of their father. The keys to a successful ghetto polygamous relationship are the same as in a regular polygamous union, and that is that the man involved must bestow upon each woman an equitable amount of love, attention, and affection. Each woman in a ghetto polygamous relationship must come to agreement with the father of child that she will only bare his children and not split up the bloodline of her children by having children with another man. Not that splitting the bloodline is such a bad thing. There may be valid reasons for the woman to cease from having children with their initial baby's father, such as genetic defects or bad genes in general. Outside of that, the woman in, this situation should consider maintaining a linear bloodline among her children by making sure they all have the same "daddy."

By doing this, she protects her child from possible domestic abuse or neglect at the hands of a new lover. Many men treat children poorly who are not genetically related to them. This often leads to severe cases of child abuse that place physiological and psychological on children that they often carry with them into adulthood. In the end though, *man-sharing* or ghetto polygamy should eventually be replaced with traditional Polygamy in order to address the severe male shortage in the black community. The African American community should sanction Polygamy, as opposed to man sharing, which often leaves the women involved at a disadvantage.

Nothing wrong with a Married man

There is nothing wrong with a married man trying to form an intimate relationship with a single woman, so long as he wants to marry her, as well. Now that is polygamy just say the word and watch how fast women run for the exit signs. *Polygamy* is the practice of the male spouse having more than one wife. Well no matter how shocking the thought of polygamy used to be in the past, today it is fast becoming an honorable alternative to extinction as an ethnic group of people. Extinction becomes a certainty when there are no surviving individuals that are able to reproduce and create a new generation. A particular group of people may become functionally extinct when only a handful of individuals survive, which are unable to reproduce due to poor health, age, sparse distribution over a large area, a lack of individuals of either sexes or other reasons. What should the black community do in response to the unbalanced sex ratios in our community? Some may suggest, celibacy, aborting female embryos, interracial marriage, lesbianism, homosexuality, etc. All of which will no doubt end with the extinction of the African American ethnic group in about 50 years. Now do not get it wrong, I am under no deluded fantasy that the modern day African-American female will come singing and dancing into the arms of polygamy. Unfortunately, many black women in American have been hardened beyond the point of return and may never be open to the understanding of what polygamy has to offer the black community. Many of them adamantly proclaim *"I ain't sharing-no-man"* and ironically many of these same "neck-rollin-rebels" usually end up with no man at all. Regardless, polygamy will balance the African American family because it is not about how many women a man can have, but it forces a man to become more responsible and diplomatic with his affections and resources. Polygamy for the African American woman teaches her how to work collectively and in harmony with other black women without feeling the need to compete.

It is funny how many black women swear never to share a man, yet this western ideology of monogamy is inherently hypocritical. Most black women have been the so-called "other woman" at least once in their lives, yet many swear that they will never share a man with another woman. Well, for the lucky few who manage not to have to share their men, the same good fortune often does not fall upon their daughters. These will ultimately grow into womanhood and face the same shortage of men as their mothers if not a worse scenario. Which is more respectable for a black woman to be? An accepted second wife or secret mistress on the side? It is time for black women in America to set the precedents in the black community that will make polygamy an honorable solution for a future generation of African American women. These generations will most certainly face the same male shortage issues that black women are facing today.

You see, monogamy is a practice of a man marrying only one woman and comes to us from the Greeks and Romans. However, what many do not understand is that many Romans who swore their loyalty to one wife nearly always had a mistress. The Greeks had a social class of warriors who so beloved their manhood so that they considered it to be more manly to bestow their affections upon other men. Greeks and Romans viewed women as nothing more than breeders. Fit only to populate their ethnic group. The Roman Republic form of government was not the only things the founders of America borrowed. The Founders of America also borrowed the customary practice of monogamy.

When it comes to African Americans the problem becomes blatantly obvious, there are simply not enough men to go around for black women. You see, globally women have always outnumbered men. This has been a part of nature's delicate balancing act when it comes to the human species. In the African American community black women outnumber black men by a larger margin than do white women out-number white men. According to Census Bureau, figures for 2002 there are nearly 2 million more black adult women than men in America a gap of 2.8 million, or 26 percent. Now considering this, we must consider black men who are gay, in jail, or die before the age of 25. We begin to see that despite many black women's fantasies, chances are they will most likely end up sharing a man one way or the other. Putting it simple, it is a mathematical impossibility for every black woman in America to have a black man all to herself.

Polygamy can help blacks economically by incorporating multiple incomes into one family unit thus thrusting black families into higher economic brackets in less than a generation. It will all but obliterate the number of children born fatherless among African Americans and erase the U.S. Census department's statistic that reads nearly 70% of African American households are headed by single black females. Polygamy will create families that are more stable and centralized around the authority of the husband and enable private educational opportunities. Opportunities such as home schooling for children who are either at risk or in need of more one-on-one attention as it pertains to their academic studies. Polygamy also acts as a safeguard against divorce because most divorces are caused by extramarital affairs. A man in a polygamous relationship already has more than one woman, so the trivial lure of other women is least likely to affect him.

Finding an honorable Married man

For many black women who are single parents, the option of getting back together with their baby's father is simply not an option for various reasons which may include issues such as incarceration, drug addiction, abuse, genetic deficiency, and so on. Therefore, for these groups of women finding a man becomes that much more challenging. Now, a small number of these women manage to find a single man to marry and become a stepfather to their child, but in most cases, many of them are forced to wait until their children are almost grown before they resume the act finding a mate. In such cases, an honorable married man who is able to lead more than one person is often the best solution. For these women, a married man brings to the table a level of maturity and leadership that a less experienced male can bring to the table. Usually a married man has children that he is either raising or has raised to adulthood. By examining his handling of their upbringing, it very easy for the single mother to see what kind of father and leader he is. If his children are unruly and disrespectful, this may tell her that he may not be an option, and that she continue looking. However, if his children are well-mannered, disciplined, productive, and courteous, then she may want to consider him as a possible option as both a husband and a father to her children. This is all dependent on whether he wants to accept such a responsibility, of course.

A single mother should look closely at how he runs his home. She needs to first pay attention to his wife and see if she is happy with him. Does his wife keep a dirty home, if so this may indicate that he has a disorganized lifestyle? Does he make his current wife happy, better, and prosperous? Any man who does not make his woman better will end up destroying her through a boring life of stale mediocrity. Does he lead his wife or does she lead him? A man led by his wife should not take on the responsibility of a polygamous relationship. The most successful polygamous relationships are often led by men who are natural born leaders because their talent for managing people, pulling them together as a cohesive unit to work together for one common goal makes them the most suitable for a polygamous style marriage. Now this is not to exclude beta males or even omega males, for that matter. It is just that polygamous marriages appeal more to the natural tendencies and talents of alpha men. Most of all, a single mother contemplating the idea of getting with a married man must first examine what she has to offer his family. Does she have a job, skill or an education? Will she be able to contribute to his household or will she be solely dependent on him for financial means. Will she be an addition to his family or will she be a distraction? If all a single mother has to offer a married man with a family is sex, she will not be around long because he already has that luxury. In other words, a single woman must be an asset to him because he will be an automatic asset to her, giving her and her child stability, leadership, and companionship. The single mother must always realize that he has a wife at home whom he loves and she needs to be happy in such a scenario as well. So the single mother must also think of how she can be an asset to his wife. In other words, she must become an asset to the married man's entire family, in order to take the relationship to the next level. At this level he actually values her as another wife and his family views her as another family member instead of an outsider or invader pulling their father/husband away from them. In order to keep from existing exclusively on the outside of this man's life, the single mother must become indispensable to his entire family.

The New Family Order

The new black family social order may consist of one or more wives and several children living together under the guidance of the husband/father. This new family structure is a "benevolent monarchy" with the eldest male operating as its leader and legal representative and speaks for the family. The power of the head of the family is supreme in the household. All must obey the head. Furthermore, the wives must obey their husbands and reverence them as kings; likewise, each husband ought to revere his wife as a queen, his daughter a princess, and his son a prince. The younger members of the family are subject to the elder members. The children must also obey and honor the parents and grandparents, and observe among themselves a law of seniority: the younger brother should obey the elder brother, and the younger sister the elder sister.

In this household all children, sons and daughters are allowed to stay at home until they are married. The family head delegates responsibilities to members according to their gifts and talents. Religious observances are the father's responsibility. The new black family unit is founded on sharing, collective contribution from each family member, entrepreneurship and a strong sense of ethnic pride. Family responsibilities take precedence over individual desires, and familial relations provide the model for social integration at all levels. In the new millennium black family structure, the individual is not so much considered as is the reputation of the family.

African American religious leaders should teach that the new black family structure preserves African American values and attitudes regardless of the moral decay and turmoil that may exist outside in the larger society. One important aspect of this family system is that the patriarchal head typically retires when he is too elderly to carry on the business affairs of the family. At this juncture, the oldest son should becomes the family head, or if the eldest son is deemed "unfit" by the father he may choose one of his younger son's to fulfill the role of "head of the family". In either case, the son must be married with children before such responsibility can be passed on to him.

In the new black family unit, the earnings of all members go into a common pool or account and the father manages the finances in this pool. Each member of the family contributes a portion of their earnings to the family pool and may use it as needed with the approval of the father. The most important role of the family is to preserve the family resources and pass them on to the next generation.

The new black family structure secures the biological continuity of the African American ethnic group, but also the cultural continuity of black society as a whole. An African American's existence should not begin simply with birth and end merely at death, but they are apart of an everlasting bloodline. They exist as part of a continuum. After death, a part of them continues to exist as long as their descendants continue to live and multiply. African Americans should no longer take pride in thinking of themselves as separate from their parents and families. Neither should they abandon their parents in their old age and turn them over to nursing homes and institutions. Instead the "new minded" African American should take responsibility for the well-being of their parents. Children are indebted to the parents and this debt lies behind the ideas of loyalty and duty; "honoring mother and father" by taking care of them in their old age by making room for them in their homes, when they are either too old or sick to take care of themselves.

The new millennium black family structure effectively conveys ideologies, customs, traditions, beliefs, and values from generation to generation, thus preserving a new African American way of life. The African American family will no longer be built on the premise of individualism, but instead collectivism. The black family stands as a unit, not fragmented. This new family order provides for African Americans a form of social security both material and psychological because members share social responsibility for the well-being of the family as a whole. This results in minimal concern over the necessities of life such as money, food, shelter, and clothing.

Collective black wealth and prosperity in America is what blacks should be striving for, so that the family is able to maintain itself without dependency on the government. You see, a nation is built on the family and economics plays a major role, insofar as it helps to establish the foundation of a family generation after generation. Well, if a family ceases to function as a family or operates dysfunctional it becomes an economic impossibility to transfer wealth.

The idea of family begins with the commitment of marriage. It is at this point that we must recognize the importance of carefully selecting the proper mate. This will ultimately assist in establishing a strong family unit. This is where most African Americans have failed miserably. A constant among the majority of blacks has been a strong spiritual inclination filtered through the religious institution of Christianity. Although, Christianity is historically a European construct, it has borrowed its core beliefs from Northeast African patriarchs. In the traditions of these biblical patriarchs, both polygamous and arranged marriages helped to build strong families with economic power and influence. African Americans need to return to these traditions that are more closely related to them culturally, than Europeanized versions of the so-called "nuclear family" structure. They must begin to rebuild the family unit by carefully choosing the mates for their children based on a system of polygamous and arranged marriages.

This type of cultural restructuring will not come without the many obstacles that for centuries have stood in the way of the proper development of the African American ethnic group. Every kind of social policy, law, and propaganda including the infamous western media has sold blacks European fairytales of monogamous romantic love and ideologies that promote an unrealistic perception of love that do not correspond to who black people really are, as a people. Instead, they entice, and invade the imagination of black folk and encourage selecting a spouse based on the slanted ideas of self-gratification and individualism. Quite simply, polygamy and arranged marriages are the only effective ways to restore and repair the black family structure that has

177

been all but destroyed during the tumultuous matriculation of African Americans through American society. The new black family structure should reflect universal order and be based on the African American core belief that G-d is the ultimate authority in the universe that creates the standards by which all living things exist. The black man must personify this authoritive role in his home, so that there is structure, accountability, and order. The word "authority" defined by Webster's dictionary means: one who has the power to influence.

The sun has authority over the earth; therefore "authority" is a universal principle and is essential for development of all living things including the fledgling black family. The Earth revolves around the Sun because of the pull or "influence" of the Sun's gravity. Gravity keeps the Earth's inhabitants from drifting into space. Gravity guides the development and growth of plants and affects the way our bones and muscles develop and function. The husband is the singular authority in his home and keeps the family from drifting apart by guiding the development and growth of those in his family through the gravity of his role as "head of household". The new black family structure should imitate this order and not be influenced by the socio-political agenda's of non-black peoples who have often preached blind morality on one hand while playing a devastating game of social, economic and political keep-away with the other.

Understanding the role of the husband

The question among many modern black women is should a man have "authority" over his wife and

178

family? The word "authority" brings the average feminist to the brink of madness. Authority, in and of itself, is meaningless without someone to submit to it. So then why is authority so important to the lives of black people? Can't or shouldn't all forms of authority be shared by all? Why should people have to submit to anything or anyone at for that matter? Why should children continue to submit to the will and guidance of their parents once they have reached an age where they can distinguish moral concepts of right and wrong? Why should anyone have to submit to employers' on the job without first being considered "equal" to them in every way first? Why should we submit to any authority without first being considered "equal" in every aspect to that authority?

Every government that assumes authority over its people imitates the order of the family. The more dysfunctional the family is, the less effective that government will be. A nation must have a strong government that will lead the people of that nation, so that order is maintained. Without order, that nation will be overrun with anarchy and remain in a constant state of chaos. In order to establish a government, the people must first "choose" a government to lead them, and then secondly, peaceably "submit" to the authority of the government that they have chosen for themselves. In the new black family structure, the husband represents the government chosen by the people and the wife represents the people who chose the government. In other words, one cannot exist without the other. Can a government exist without a people to govern? Can a people exist in peace without a government to maintain order?

Can the modern black man exist without a black woman to empower him, and likewise can the modern black women continue to exist without a black man to lead her? This is the balance of mutual respect between the sexes in the new black family household. When men and women refuse to ascribe to these universal principles, they are ultimately opening the door to anarchy into their communities. Humans are the only species of mammal that have the ability to think critically about their own existence. This critical thinking ability often causes them to resist natural laws that govern their existence. It is the task of African Americans to bring their passions inline with nature's order. No matter how hard people try to out-think nature's law, in the end humans must submit to it or risk a self-imposed extinction as a particular ethnic group.

Basic principles of the New Millennium African American family:

1. Every member sees to the needs of his family member before his own needs
2. The family bares the burdens of the weakest members.
3. Members do not "loan" money to each other, instead they give what is needed without expectation of repayment
4. All in the family concur that there is but one G-d.
5. Every member insures the integrity of the family by demonstrating good character.
6. Each member of the family values the opinions and ideas of the other.
7. To honor one's parents is to honor G-d.
8. Each family member understands that the father/husband is the leader of that family and his authority governs the household.

Family Structure

Women are the basis of new black family structure. They are Queens, mothers, and educated. This new type of black American society is considered Matrilineal and not Matriarchal because the African American man is the dominant one who runs the family. Both African American men and women need to be a part of a strong family unit. African American women have the innate ability to survive independently however; they can only truly succeed and thrive as members of a family group. In this new family structured community, the woman has the right to own property and to be educated, so long as she is willing

181

to submit all of her gifts, talents, and resources to her husband with the understanding that he is her leader, protector, and spiritual covering.

The new black family unit will be successful because of a collective effort on the part of each immediate family member to contribute his or her abilities to obtain wealth and resources. As a whole, this gives the new black family greater economic rewards. Numbers are important here because the larger the new black family becomes the greater the material success.

If a man has more than one wife, then the women should cooperate in raising the children. Each wife should help to raise each child. The wife who bares the husband his first-born son is the "first" wife. Her role is that of Queen of the household because a man's firstborn son is a genetic continuation of himself passing along his paternal bloodline. Thus, the woman who manages to be the first to give a man the opportunity to continue his legacy beyond his lifetime should be respected and her place in his life should forever be secure. Other wives respect the first wife. The authority of the first wife extends to the rest of household, only the husband is exempt from her authority. It is the duty of the first wife to synchronize the other wives into one cohesive unit. This will work towards the benefit of the entire household. The first wife does not "rule" over the other wives. She is not their authority the husband is, however; she manages the contributions of the other wife or wives to the household. If the husband wields power and influence over others outside of his home, then the first son has the right then the first son has the right to his seat upon his death or retirement. If the husband is a common man or a man strictly of economic wealth, then he should distribute his wealth equally among all of his children upon his death or retirement.

Arranged Marriage and the New Black Family

Arranged marriage or the word "betrothal" literally means "a mutual promise or contract for a future marriage." Arranged marriages are not spontaneous occurrences. In the ancient Northeast African traditions, one could be betrothed to a future spouse as early as the age of 13 years old. Marital arrangement was established as a permanent part of the marriage process in order to insure generational stability both economically and socially. Arrangement helps the individual to do away with the needless guessing game of marriage. Children who are arranged to a future spouse spend less time "on the hunt" for that special someone because that someone is already being prepared for them by their parents. They spend less time frequenting clubs, bars, and single scenes and devote more time to trades, life skills, and or academic studies. African American children would have a greater chance at success because after being arranged at an early age, focusing on a more productive lifestyle becomes a priority.

Marital arrangement is established in one of several ways. When it is time for a man and woman to marry, both heads of the two respective families negotiate financial terms of the union in order to compensate the bride-to-be's family because she is considered a valuable asset to her family. After coming to a mutual agreement of marriage, the couple is formally engaged and a formal engagement contract is drawn up binding the agreement between the two families. During this time, the young man's family is responsible for providing a place for the couple to live. Only after a suitable place for them to live has been obtained can the marriage actually take place. This ensures that the marriage has a decent head start economically and is not handicapped by lack of proper living conditions. While the young man's family is securing the living conditions, the bride-to-be would remain at her parents' home learning how to be a wife from elder women in her family. Betrothal could be a valuable tool for African American families seeking to restore their family structure. It can help them navigate more freely through the murky waters of reckless dating in modern society. It can also help African Americans create stronger family bonds that are able to perpetuate family wealth and privilege with each generation. Arranged marriages ensure that "selfishness" is never apart of the decision-making process. This kind of grooming should begin with black children at the age of 13, in order to properly prepare them for marriage. This type of marital preparation helps to develop our young people into good husbands and wives it helps to eradicate dysfunctional homes. The concept of randomized dating or courting should no longer be endorsed or practiced by the new black family. Instead, black children should be reared to believe in family first. Marriage is a social and economic necessity for the African American family in America because it is the basis of any community. It is also the means of preserving and continuing the human race. Marriage fortifies the bonds between families and communities by maintaining a proper lineage. This change in lifestyle among black Americans ensures that each newborn child can identify with both a mother and a father without confusion, thus maintaining a proper social order in the black community.

Husband's duty

The husband must provide a vision for his wife and family that will ensure the wife's incontestable right to a home, clothing, nourishing, and general care and well being. The wife's residence must be adequate to provide a reasonable level of privacy, comfort, and independence. His wife should have other rights of a moral nature as well. A husband must treat his wife with equity, respect her feelings, and show her kindness and consideration. The husband should show her no aversion, nor should she be subjected to suspense and uncertainty. No man should be allowed to keep his wife with the intention of abusing her or hindering her freedom.

Wife's duty

These are the wife's duties to her husband. The wife must be faithful, trustworthy, and honest. She must not be deceitful in any way towards her husband and her home. Nor must she allow any other person to have access to sexual intimacy, which is her husband's exclusive right. She must not receive or entertain strange males in her home, nor may she accept their gifts. This prevents jealousy, suspicion, gossip, etc., and helps maintain the integrity of her household. With respect to intimacy, the wife should make herself desirable and attractive. She should also be responsive, and cooperative. A wife should not withhold herself from her husband. The wife should not do anything that may render her companionship less desirable or less gratifying. The husband's possessions are her trust. She should not lend or dispose of any of his belongings without his permission.

What about Divorce?

The new black family unit should no longer marry with the notion of divorce as a back-up plan. Divorce should only be considered only in the extreme cases where abuse and adultery are present.

Practical strategies for Arranged marriage

Frankly, the previously discussed arranged marriage strategy is idyllic at best. However, a more practical implementation of arranged marriages can be practiced as a form of "networking" among African Americans. With such technologies at our disposal such as DNA testing, it has become a lot easier to play matchmaker when it comes to arranging proper unions for black children. Through such technological advancements, it is possible to screen people before marriage. All it takes is for African Americans with children who are familiar with each other to start to match-make their children informally based on social and economic commonality and opportunity.

The absence of strong marriages in the black community has resulted in the infestation of crime, violence, disease, and social decadence that is ravaging our communities and killing our children. Whenever the institution of marriage is "sick." society, as a whole, becomes sick. If there were no such thing as marriage, there would be no order in the world whatsoever, and the world would be plunged into chaos. The new black family should be a practical community grounded in reality, recognizing that human sexual desire is a natural part of the human experience. Sexual desire should be supported within a proper family structure. Extreme vows of sexual abstinence by men and women who are eligible to marry are inconsistent with the functioning of the family and lend opportunity for deviant sexual behavior. Marriage is a moral safeguard against hedonism and social decadence. Alternative relationships such as open marriage, swinging couples, spouse swapping, and other

187

decadent practices should never be recognized as legitimate life styles by the new black family unit. Sexual relations through these arrangements are unethical and counterproductive to the restoration of the black family in America.

The Old Concept of American style dating

The new black family unit should no longer practice casual dating between unmarried couples. Still, if one does not date as is practiced in Western society how do they decide whom to marry? This is a common question among many people. "Dating," as it is termed in Western society occurs when a young man and woman engage in a one-on-one intimate relationship, spending time together alone, "getting to know each other" in a very deep way. This is done before deciding whether that is the person, they will marry. A casual sexual relationship between the two is normally an aspect of this process, as well.

As currently practiced in American society, casual unsupervised dating or courting has been a very self-destructive practice for black Americans and has yielded little if any positive or productive results. Instead, in most cases this form of reckless behavior has led to an increase in emotionally damaged females who often grow into bitter adult women heading single-parent homes due to premature teen pregnancy. It has also led to dramatic increases in sexually transmitted diseases, namely HIV infection, which is killing more black women each day. The choice of a marriage partner is one of the most important decisions a person will make in life. It should not be taken lightly or left to chance. It should be given careful consideration, investigation and proper family planning. So in today's world, how do young people manage? The answer lies in giving them the proper framework in which to live. Here are some basic guidelines for the arranged marriage process:

1. African Americans looking for a spouse should weigh the matter heavily these days.

2. The family enquires, discusses, and suggests candidates. They consult with each other to narrow down potential prospects. The leaders of both families meet to suggest a possible arrangement.

3. The couple agrees to meet in a chaperoned group environment. The family investigates the character of the candidate by interviewing friends of the candidate.

4. Candidates for marriage should be given the freedom to choose whether they are pleased with the marriage arrangement and should not be forced into a marriage.

5. The African American father should have the right to give his daughter's hand in marriage to a man that he approves. The daughter should not simply marry whomsoever she wishes, but she should be able to choose not to marry one who is chosen for her and request of her father to choose another candidate. This kind of marriage preparation helps to ensure the foundation of the marriage, by utilizing the wisdom of family elders. Family involvement in the marriage selection process helps to assure that the choice is based on a careful, objective evaluation of the compatibility of the couple.

189

Tackling the man shortage

THE 2004 RACIAL INDEX

1. *More black men than black women are born each year*
   606,000: number of black births in 2001
   308,575: number of black males born in 1985
   299,618: number of black females born in 1985
   23: percentage of black births to teenage mothers, in 1990
   18.9: percentage of black births to teenage mothers, in 2001

2. *Women are the majority of the black population*
   36 million: total black population in March 2002   19.3 million: black female population in March 2002   16.7 million: black male population in March 2002   53.6: Percentage of black population that is female

3. *There are 2.7 million more black women than black men.*
   24.3 million: total black adult population in March 2002
   13.5 million: total black female adult population in March 2002
   10.8 million: total black male adult population in March 2002
   55.5: Percentage of black adults who are female

As a community, African Americans are going to have to start making small concessions when it comes to trivial social taboos such as age. What I mean by this is that in modern society today, it is looked down upon for a younger woman to have an intimate relationship with a man significantly older. Men interested in forming an intimate relationship with a younger woman or marrying age are tagged with such labels as:

"Chester the molester," perverts, and dirty old men. There is no clear reason why this idiotic form of thinking exists. This kind of social stigmatism eliminates nearly all eligible black men who are actually capable of sustaining a family economically. Once a woman turns 18 years old, she is legally considered an adult in most states and other civilized countries in the world as well. So why then, do we expect them to avoid older men and simply date and marry "boys" their age? If you really look at it, this kind of groundless thinking is setting many black women up for failure at an early age. For younger women, the only socially acceptable males available to them are underdeveloped males who often live with their parents and have no resources economically, or otherwise, to sustain any "real" relationship with the opposite sex. 18-year-old women, left with such a limited to pool of black men, are having sex with these underdeveloped males and in many cases getting pregnant by them in record numbers. This has led to the high number of single parent homes in the black community. Marriage between two 18-year-olds is so uncommon these days, that it almost never happens, and those that do usually divorce by the age of 25 because of financial hardships.

So what is an 18-year-old woman to do? As a community, African Americans need to socially accept and promote the idea that an 18-year-old woman who is sexually active needs to be introduced to a more eligible pool of black men who are more stable minded and financially secure. These types of men usually tend to be at least ten to twenty years older than the average 18 year-old-female. They have more education, job stability, and economic resources than average males her age or slightly older. Pairing an 18-year-old black woman with a black man who is at least 28 years old increases the probability of a successful marriage. It will economically secure family structure, because she is dealing with a more mature man. An older man has already gone through the major stages of social, mental, and economic development that boys her age or slightly older have yet to complete. Thus, she is not handicapped by his lack of development, but instead, she and any resulting offspring are enhanced by his experience. These children are not automatic welfare babies from birth.

Black men between the ages of 15 and 25 have very little, if anything, to offer a woman. Outside of sex and social companionship unless they come from an economically advantaged family there is little. Outside of that, these undeveloped men are nothing more than a liability to a young 18-year-old woman. These men need grooming and extensive training by older men on how to become responsible leaders and productive providers. Once these men are at least 28 years old, ten years older than the 18-year-old African American female, they are ready to be suitable options for her to choose as a husband. Black men between the ages of 17 and 25 who grew up in fatherless homes with no respectable male figures to emulate or to groom them would be best served by joining the military. They should enroll in its leadership programs, so that they will at least learn a well-defined concept of how to become a leader in some sense.

The bottom line is our young women need black men to become leaders, so that they can become better fathers and husbands. African American men who are leaders can reverse the negative disfunctionality that has plagued black families in America since the days of slavery.

End Game

Many black people today do not have a reference point on where to begin starting a relationship. Usually a person gathers the information necessary to form a solid marriage from their experiences as a child, witnessing their parents carry on the business of sustaining a marriage. This childhood experience usually involves being exposed to male authority, leadership, love, and protection. Without this experience, both male and female children get only one side of the equation when it comes to dealing with the opposite sex in an intimate relationship. Without this exposure, to the male side of things, both male and female children grow up insecure about relationships period. You see the number one thing that a man brings to a relationship is a "standard" and his standard becomes the law of his home. This standard instills in each child a sense of accountability. This helps to police their natural desire to be self-absorbed and reckless.

Without the presence of the father Macks, Players and Snakes evolve from a generation of young boys who would otherwise become fathers and husbands. These individuals often wreak havoc within intimate relationships because all are driven by deep-rooted insecurities that usually are evident of a dysfunctional family background where there was no emphasis on leadership and responsibility. The havoc these men wreak usually has a scarring effect on the hearts of the women they come into contact with creating negative baggage for them to carry on to the next relationship. Without the presence of the father, Queen B's, Hoes, and Freaks evolve from little girls who would otherwise become mothers and wives.

194

These types of women have a negative effect on black relationships because they normally live a lifestyle with multiple sex partners and help to perpetuate the cycle of dysfunctionality by getting pregnant by more than one man. The problem with black relationships is the "family" and the problem with the family is "no leadership." African Americans cannot continue to exist depending solely on the black woman. Black female matriarchy was forced upon African Americans from the very beginning and should not be expected to sustain the black race in America into the future. The problems that I have outlined in this book are systemic within the black community because black families are weak or non-existent.

The solutions are extremely hard to digest for some people. However, until the black family is restored, African Americans will continue to form unhealthy relationships that breed hostility, uncertainty, and economic instability. There can be no "restoration" of the black family structure without first restoring the black man to his rightful place as "leader" of his family. The society in which we live has undermined black male leadership within black relationships so much that it has almost taken its entire toll on the relationship between the black man and his woman. The reason why black men and women cannot seem to "get it together" when it comes to forming families is that we have too many negative social elements that are counterproductive to such organization.

Slavery, social welfare, and feminism have all been tools used to help dismantle the black family, and it is going to take a conscious effort on behalf of blacks to undo the problems created by those tools. The family

195

is an institution that humans use as a safety net in order to survive and prosper. Without it, we are weak and vulnerable to outside forces that would threaten our very existence. The phrase "black family" is almost an oxymoron, because it contradicts the majority of black people's reality. The majority of black "so called" families are single parent homes, thus rendering them inherently dysfunctional. Without the father present, black children grow up half-prepared to deal with being "whole" or one with a spouse in a marriage. Single parent homes breed children who lack respect for authority and view the opposite sex as an invader, rather than a partner. The father/husband establishes the "rules of the game" that ultimately bring "order" to the family.

The mother/wife nourishes and supports the leadership of her husband by being the first to respect his leadership. By doing this, she empowers him as her King and ordains herself his Queen, thus they both establish a kingdom (family) together that is based on a mutual dependency. He depends on her acknowledgement of his leadership to become King for without a Queen to submit to his leadership he has nothing to rule. She, in turn, depends on his leadership to maintain order and prosperity in a kingdom that she gives birth to. This true balance must exist between black men and women in order to maintain healthy relationships, as well as strong families. Once black folk realize this, we will not only be able to "get it together." but when it comes to love relationships, we will also be able to "get together and stay together."

Bibliography

Alexander, A. (n.d). How I discovered my grandmother and the truth about Black women and the suffrage movement. *African sense of western gender discourses.* Minneapolis: University of Minnesota Press.

Almeida, D. M., Wethington, E., & McDonald, D. A. (2001). Daily variation in paternal engagement and negative mood: Implications for emotionally supportive and conflictual interactions. *Journal of Marriage and the Family.*

Andersson, G. (2001). The motives of foster parents, their family and work circumstances. *British Journal of Social Work*

Aptheker, B. (1982). *Woman's Legacy: Essays on Race, Sex, and Class in American History* Amherst, MA: University of Massachusetts.

Ball, Edward. (1998). *Slaves in the Family.* New York: Farrar, Straus and Giroux.

Bates, K. G. (1996). *Basic Black: Home Training for Modern Times.* New York: Doubleday.

Berkeley, K. C. (1985). Colored ladies also contributed: Black Women's Activities from Benevolence to Social Welfare, 1866-1896. In Walter J. Fraser, Jr. (ed.), *Web of Southern Social Relations: Women, Family, & Education.* .Athens, GA: University of GA Press.

Blair, K. J. (1980).*The Clubwoman as Feminist: True Womanhood Redefined, 1868-1914** New York: Holmes & Meier, 1980

Bower-Russa, M. E., Knutson, J. F., & Winebarger, A. (2001). Disciplinary history, adult disciplinary attitudes, and risk for abusive parenting.

Butts, J. D. (1981). Adolescent Sexuality and Teenage Pregnancy from a Black Perspective . In T. Ooms (ed.), *Teenage Pregnancy in a Family Context,* Philadelphia: Temple University Press.

Casper, L.M., and Fields, J. (2000).*Americas Families and Living Arrangements: Population Characteristics.* United States Census Bureau.

Catt, C. H. and Rogers, N. S. (1969). *Woman Suffrage and Politics.* Seattle: University of Washington Press.

Greth, C. V (1951). The Spirit of Women. *The Austin American Statesman.*

Cash, F. L. B. (1986). *Womanhood and protest: The club movement among black women. 1892-1922. "* Ph.D. dissertation. SUNY/Stony Brook.

Collins, P. H. (1991). The Meaning of Motherhood in Black Culture. In R. Staples (4th ed.), *The Black Family.* Belmont, Calif: Wadsworth Publishing Co.

Coleman, C. (1997). *Mama Knows Best.* New York: Simon & Schuster.

Coleman, Willie Mae. (1982). *Keeping the Faith and Disturbing the Peace: Black Women from Anti-slavery to Women's Suffrage.* Ph.D. dissertation, University of CA/Irvine.

Cottman, M. H. (1996). *Family of Black America.* New York: Crown.

Crouter, A. C., Bumpus, M. F., Head, M. R., & McHale, S. M. (2001). Implications of overwork and overload for the quality of men's family relationships. *Journal of Marriage and the Family.*

Neverdon-Morton, C. *The black woman's struggle for equality in the south 1895-1925.*

Daly, K. J. (2001). Deconstructing family time: from ideology to lived experience. *Journal of Marriage and the Family*

Davis, A. (1981). *Women, race, & class.* New York: Random House.

Davis, L. G. and Daniels, B. S. (1981). *Black athletes in the United States: A bibliography of books, articles, autobiographies and biographies on black professional athletes in the U.S., 1800-1981.* Westport, CT: Greenwood Press.

Davis, L. G. (1986).*The black family in the U.S.: A revised, updated, selectively annotated bibliography.* New York: Greenwood Press.

Davis, N. (1985). *Afro-American reference: An annotated bibliography of selected resources.* Westport, CT: Greenwood Press.

Deniz K. (1994). Identity and Its Discontents: Women and the Nation. In Patrick Williams and Laura Chrisman (Eds.), *Colonial Discourse and Post-Colonial Theory.* New York: Columbia University Press. (p. 378).

Dialectics and Gender: Anthropological approaches. Boulder: Westview Press.

Diggs, Anita Doreen. (1998). *Staying married: A guide for African American couples.* New York: Kensington Books.

Dillaway, H., & Broman, C. (2001). Race, class, and gender differences in marital satisfaction and divisions of household labor among dual-earner couples: A case for intersectional analysis. *Journal of Family Issues.*

Domitrovich, C. E., & Bierman, K. L. (2001). Parenting practices and child social adjustment: multiple pathways of influence.

A History of Women in the West. In George Duby & Michelle Perrot (Eds.), *Ancient Goddesses to Christian Saints.* (1994). Boston: Harvard University Press.

Early, G. (1994). *Daughters: On family & fatherhood.* Reading, Mass.: Addison Wesley Longman, 1994.

E. B. Barnett [Higginbotham]. (1996). Nannie Burroughs and the education of black women. *Faith of Our Fathers: African-American men reflect on fatherhood.* New York: Dutton.

*Father Songs: Testimonies by African American sons & daughters. (*1997). Boston: Beacon Press.

Feminism and Suffrage. (1980). Ithaca, N.Y: Cornell University Press.

Fox, G. L., & Bruce, C. (2001). Conditional fatherhood: Identity theory and parental investment theory as alternative sources of explanation of fathering. *Journal of Marriage and the Family*

Franklin, D. L. (1997). Ensuring inequality: The structural transformation of the African-American family. New York: Oxford University Press.

Furstenberg, F. F., & Kiernan, K. E. (2001). Delayed parental divorce: How much do children benefit? *Journal of Marriage and the Family.*

Gero, J.M. ja M.W.Conkey, (Eds.), (1991). *Engendering archaeology: Women and prehistory.* Oxford: Basil Blackwell.

Gerda Lerner. (1986). *The Creation of Patriarchy.* New York: Oxford University Press.

Giddings, P. (1984). *When and where I enter: The impact of black women on race and sex in America** New York: Wm. Morrow.

Gilkes, C. T. *Successful rebellious professional: The black woman's professional identity and Community commitment.*

Gimbutas, M. (1991). *The civilization of the goddess. The world of old Europe. San* Francisco: Harper.

Gowdy, J. (1999). Hunter-gatherers and the mythology of the market. of hunters and gatherers. *Cambridge Encyclopedia.* Cambridge University Press.

Greenwood Press. (1980). The first major bibliography on the Afro-American Woman covering all subject areas, since Lenwood Davis' annotated bibliography, *The Black Woman in American Society.*

Guo, G., & Harris, K. M. (2000). The mechanisms mediating the effects of poverty on children's intellectual development.

Gutman, H. (1976). *The Black family: From slavery to freedom.* New York: Pantheon.

Gutman, Herbert George. (1977). *Black family in slavery and freedom, 1750-1925.* New York: Random House.

Han, W., Waldfogel, J., & Brooks-Gunn, J. (2001). The effects of early maternal employment on later cognitive and behavioral outcomes. *Journal of Marriage and the Family*

Harley, S. & R. Terborg- Penn (eds.), (1978).*The Afro American woman's struggles and images* Pt. Washington, NY: Kennikat.

Martineau, H. (1837). *Society in America. Vol. 1.* New York: Saunders & Otley.

Hedgeman, A. A. (1964). The trumpet sounds: A memoir of Negro leadership. New York: Holt Rinehart

Higginbotham, E. B. (1990). In Politics to Stay: Black Women Leaders and Party Politics in the 1920s. In Louise Tilly and Patricia Gurin (Eds.), *Women, Politics, and Change.*

Hine, D. C. *When the truth is told: A history of Black women's culture and community in Indiana, 1875-1950.*

Hine, D. C., Wilma King, & Reed, L. (eds.), "We Specialize in the Wholly Impossible: A Reader in Black Women's History

Hull, G., P. Scott, & Smith, B. (Eds.), *But some of us Are brave: Black women's studies*

Hooks, Bell, *Ain't I a woman: Black women and feminism*

Hrabowski, F. (1998). *Beating the odds: Raising academically successful African-American males.* New York: Oxford University Press.

Hutchinson, Earl Ofari. (1994). *Black fatherhood II: Black women talk about their men.* Los Angeles: Middle Passage Press.

Hutton, Mary Magdelene Boone. (1975). *The rhetoric of Ida B. Wells: The genesis of the anti-lynch movement,"* Ph.D. dissertation, Indiana University.

Jenkins, M. T. (1984). *The history of the black woman's club movement in America.* Ph.D. dissertation, Columbia University/Teachers College.

Jolly, M. and Macintyre, M. (Eds.), 1989. *Family and gender in the Pacific. Domestic.* contradictions *and the colonial impact.* Cambridge: Cambridge University Press.

Johnson, H. D., LaVoie, J. C., & Mahoney, M. (2001). Interparental conflict and family cohesion: Predictors of loneliness, social anxiety, and social avoidance in late adolescence.

Jones, A Lash, Jane E. H.: A Case Study of Black Leadership, 1910-1 950.

Jones, J, Labor of Love, Labor of Sorrow: Black Women, Work, and the Family, From Slavery to Present

Kamla B. 1993. What is Patriarchy? New Delhi: Kali for Women; Uma Chakravarti. 1993.

King, K. L. (ed) 1997 Women and Goddess Traditions. In Antiquity and today. Minneapolis: Fortress Press.

Kunjufu, J. (1996). Restoring the Village, Values and Commitment: Solutions for the Black Family. Chicago Ill.: African American Images.

Lawrence III, C. (1992). Cringing at the Myths of Black Sexuality. In R. Chrisman, & R. Allen (eds.), Court of Appeal: *The Black Community Speaks Out on the Racial and Sexual Politics of Clarence Thomas vs. Anita Hill,*New York: Ballantine.

Lepowsky, M. (1990). Gender in an Egalitarian Society: A case study from the Coral Sea. in Sanday and Goodenough.

Lerner, G. (1986). The creation of patriarchy. New York: Oxford University Press.

Lerner, G. The Grimke Sisters from South Carolina.

Gordon, L. Woman's Body, Woman's Right (New York: Penguin Books, Inc., 1976)

Lifting the Veil, Shattering the Silence: Black Women's History in Slavery and Freedom," in Hine, (ed.), *The State of Afro-American History: Past, Present and Future.*

Longmore, M. A., Manning, W. D., & Giordano, P. C. (2001). Preadolescent parenting strategies and teens' dating and sexual initiation: A longitudinal analysis. *Journal of Marriage and the Family.*

M. G. Smith. (1966). A Survey of West Indian Family Studies," in Edith Clarke, My Mother Who Fathered Me: *A Study of the Family in Three Selected Communities in Jamaica, (2nd ed.).* London: George Allen and Unwin.

Madhubuti, Haki. *Black Men Obsolete, Single, Dangerous?: Afrikan American families in Transition.* Chicago: Third World Press, 1990.

Maurer, T. W., Pleck, J. H., & Rane, T. R. (2001). *Parental identity and reflected-appraisals: measurement and gender dynamics.*

Mead, M. (1962). *Male and female. A study of sexes in a changing world.* Penguin Books.

Momsen. 1993. Ibid.:233; Peake. 1993.

Naomi Goldenberg (1979). *Changing of the Gods: Feminism and the End of Traditional Religions* (Boston.: Beacon Press.

O'Sullivan, L. F., Meyer-Bahlburg, H. F. L., & Watkins, B. X. (2001). Mother-daughter communication about sex among urban African American and Latino families. *Journal of Adolescent Research*

Oyewumi, O. 1997. *The Invention of Women. Making an African sense of Western gender discourses.* Minneapolis: University of Minnesota Press.

Parker, L., & Allen, T. D. (2001). Work/ family benefits: Variables related to employee's fairness perceptions. *Journal of Vocational Behavior*

Personal recollection of Harry Singh in New York, December1995. Interview with Gora Singh, 1996. Phyllis Zagano, "In Whose Image? - *Feminist Theology at the Crossroads,* "This World (Fall, 1986)

Punamaki, R. (2001). From childhood trauma to adult well-being through psychosocial assistance of Chilean families.

Quest for Equality: The Life and Writings of Mary Eliza Church Terrell, 1863-1 954 Quoted in William L. O'Neill, *Everyone was Brave: A History of Feminism in America* New York: Quadrant Press, (1971).

Raising Black Children in a Turbulent World. New York: Anchor Books, (1996).

Reiter, R. R., (ed.) (1975). *Toward an anthropology of women.* New York: Monthly Review press.

Righteous Discontent: The Woman's Movement in the Black Baptist Church* (1993). Cambridge: Harvard.

Rogers, S. J., DeBoer, D. D. (2001). Changes in wives' income: Effects on marital happiness, psychological well-being, and the risk of divorce.

Røkkum, A. 1998. Goddesses, priestesses, and sisters. Mind, gender, and power in the monarchic tradition of the Ryukyus. Oslo. Scandinavian University Press.

Roslyn Terborg-Penn, "Discrimination Against Afro-American Women in the Women's Movement, 1830-1920,"

Sahlins, M. 1985. Islands of history. Chicago University Press.

Sanday, P. R. and Ruth Gallagher Goodenough, editors. (1990). *Beyond the second sex: new direction in the anthropology of gender.* Philadelphia: University of Pennsylvania Press.

Sarah Grimke. (1837) *Letters on the Equality of the Sexes and the Condition of Woman LetterXII* New York: Burt Franklin.

Shek, D. T. (2001). Paternal and maternal influences on family functioning among Hong Kong Chinese families. Simpson, Rennie (1983). "The Afro-American Female: The Historical Context of the Construction of Sexual Identity." In Snitow, Ann [and others], (Eds.), *Powers of Desire: The Politics of Sexuality.* New York: Monthly Review Press.

Sims-Wood, J. L. The Progress of Afro-American Women: A Selected Bibliography and Resource Guide. Westport, CN: Greenwood Press, 1980. (MCK STACKS also) The first major bibliography on the Afro-American Woman covering all subject areas, since Lenwood Davis' annotated bibliography, *The Black Woman in American Society.*

Singletary, M. *Daddy's home at last: What It Takes For Dads to Put Families First.* Grand Rapids, MI: Zondervan Publishing House, 1998.

Sonia L. N, "Is Goddess Worship Finally Going to Put Men in Their Place?" The Wall Street Journal, June 7,1990, A1.

Staples, R., & Johnson, L. B. (1993). *Black Families at the Crossroads: Challenges and Prospects.* San Francisco, CA: Jossey- Bass Publishers

Stevens, D., Kiger, G., & Riley, P. J. (2001). *Working hard and hardly working: domestic labor and marital*

Susan B. Anthony, Elizabeth Cady Stanton, and Ida H. Harper(1881).*The History of Woman Suffrage*, Vol. 1 New York: Fowler & Wells.

Thomsen, E., Mosley, J., Hanson, T. L., & McLanahan, S. S. (2001). *Remarriage, cohabitation, and changes in mothering behavior.*

Thornton, Yvonne S. DitchDigger's Daughters: A Black Family?s *Astonishing Success.* Story. New York: Plume, 1995.

Tsushima, T., & Gecas, V. (2001). Role taking and socialization in single- parent families

Tucker, M. B., & Taylor, R. J. (1989). Demographic Correlates of Relationship Status among Black Americans. *Journal of Marriage and the Family.* "'We Specialize in the Wholly Impossible': The Philanthropic Work of Black Women," in Kathleen D. McCarthy, (ed.),

Lady Bountiful Revisited: Women, Philanthropy, and Power

White, J., & Parham, T. (1990). *The Psychology of Blacks: An African- American Perspective.* (2nd ed.), Englewood Cliffs, N.J.: Prentice-Hall.

Wilson, P. (1986, March). Black Culture and Sexuality. Journal of Social Work and Human Sexuality

Wyatt, G., & Lyons-Rowe, S. (1990, April). African American Women's Sexual Satisfaction as a Dimension of their Sex Roles. *Sex Roles.*

Wyatt, G. et al. (1988, August). Kinsey Revisited II: Comparisons of the Sexual Socialization and Sexual Socialization and Sexual Behavior of Black Women over 33 Years. *Archives of Sexual Behavior*

Whitley, D. M., Kelley, S. J., & Sipe, T. A. (2001). Grandmothers raising grandchildren: Are they at increased risk of health problems